MUSIC MAN

1978 to 1982 (and then some)!!

The Other Side of the Story

By Frank W/M Green

With Leo Fender, TOM WALKER, Forrest White, The Ernie Ball Family , Babe Simoni, George Fullerton, Uschi Eastman, Elizabeth Pedraza Meyer, Mark Wentling, Jody Carver, Jack Steele, John Chelchowski, Bud Driver and a cast of thousands!!

Acknowledgements: To my family for their support; Deirdre Ann, Michael, Linda,Tom Sargent and to Ron Middlebrook/Centerstream for his encouragement.

ISBN 13: 978-1-57424-216-4
ISBN 10: 1-57424-216-4
SAN: 683-8022

CENTERSTREAM

Table of Contents

MUSIC MAN

MUSIC MAN

Forward

Music Man 1978 to 1982

Music Man, 1978 to 1982, was like a brilliant comet of music-driven energy and technical innovation that flashed across the heavens viewed by guitar-gazers around the world.

Music Man traced a magnificent orbit in its first go-round, launched by a veteran team; Leo Fender, Forrest White and Chief Pilot/Navigator, Tom Walker.

Music historians have treated these three industry pioneers and their associates in different degrees. Each of them had many friends and loyal supporters. Leo Fender, of course, is deservedly the front runner, by virtue of his 'founding father' image of the solid body guitar. Forrest White was in the' right place at the right time' to be recognized for his manufacturing contributions. Tom Walker, on the other hand, has not received credit for his genius in the designs and improvements he master minded for guitar and bass amplification. Music Man was his inspiration! Included herein, is a 'Tribute to Tom Walker', a fine gentleman and a true friend.

This book deals primarily with four years, 1978 to 1982. 'And Then Some" turns the ball (pun intended), over to Ernie and family.

There will always be a Music Man!!

Respectfully,

Frank W/M Green
with Mark Wentling, Jody Carver, Babe Simoni

Introduction

I met TOM WALKER when I was eleven years old, in the summer of 1954. I was Ernie Ball's first steel guitar student. At the time, Tom was the sales rep for Fender Musical Instruments and Fender was producing a yearly national contest of students known as National Music Association. (NMA) Music Stores with lesson programs brought their students from all over America to compete. A trade show was included as part of the event, which took place at Long Beach Civic Auditorium. Few people know Tom's history of the NMA and of how many young student's lives were affected in a positive way during the fifteen years of NMA event existence.

Tom and Ernie Ball were best friends for all of their lives. He was Godfather to Ernie and wife, Novagale's children; Sherwood, David, Sterling and Nova. He was well-known in the Music Trades for his Dealer support and helpfulness. Tom was my friend, of the highest integrity and favorite-of-all reps. CBS bought Fender in 1965. Leo was retained as a consultant, but soon became disenchanted. He, Tom and other principals of the original Fender group left CBS. There was an additional five year clause restricting Leo from active involvement in the music industry. Leo, Tom and Forrest White were very unhappy with CBS handling of product quality control bearing the Fender name. They formed a research team and bided their time. Thus began the ground work for MUSIC MAN!

Tom introduced Music Man amps while Leo made the guitars and basses. Music Man amps were designed by Tom and were the best available; the first to combine solid state and tubes together. Tom Walker was the heart and soul of the new venture. He will always be remembered as a loyal friend and 'Music Man'!!

Respectfully,
J.T.
Johnny Thompson Music
Monterey Park, California.

Pictured at an *MFE meeting on May 11th, 2005, left to right: Johnny Thompson, Todd Trent and Rob DeKarr. *MFE (Music For Everyone) is a group of Music Retailers who meet monthly, dedicated to the surviving and thriving of the independent Music Store!

Chapter 1

Fender, Tom Walker and Music Man

The time was the 1960's. The store was Music For Everyone in Sierra Madre, California. Any thing that looked like a solid- body guitar was called a 'Fender' by the unenlightened. The in-crowd knew all about 'real' Fenders. There were no other preferences in their guitar related vocabulary. The evolution of Music For Everyone had missed the mark. Berry and Grassmueck and The Arcadia Music Mart in the neighboring cities, big stores by comparison, both had the Fender line.

Music For Everyone was serviced by four of the legendary sales reps who supplied us with our major lines. They were: Frank Garlock, Standel; Ray Ortega, Coast Wholesale (then distributing Martin); Tiny Timbrell, Gibson and Jack Steele, Pacific Music Supply (then carrying Guild). Pressure from the always critical youthful segment of our customer base kept taunting, "if you don't have Fender, you're an un-cool store"! Not that I was influenced by them but, what the heck, I'll give Fender a call!

At that time the fifth legendary and highly respected rep was Tom Walker, of Fender Musical Instruments. I had never met Tom, nor was I going to for another nine or ten years. A phone call to Fender was taken by a receptionist and I, told that Tom Walker was somewhere out on the road. I was to leave my name, phone number and store location. He would get back to me upon his return.

Grappling with the responsibilities of a retail music store over fourteen years, was always an all-consuming, round-the-clock challenge. Returning to other pursuits, the Fender inquiry left my mind. When CBS bought Fender, rumblings of product quality dissatisfaction funneled through out the industry. Leo Fender and those loyal to him were gone. The new glitz and hype group thought that advertizing alone was the key to a successful musical instrument line. You could look good to stockholders by building a cheaper product, sacrificing performance for profit margins. Most of the new marketing experts at CBS were not guitar players.

The problem was that musicians knew the difference and wouldn't buy superficial look-a-likes. To Leo and his close associates, this was a direct personal disgrace to the Fender name. Leo, himself, couldn't publicly do any thing about it until his agreement with CBS fulfilled the time limit requirements of his contract. He could, however, talk with Forrest and Tom about new and better instruments for a future venture.

Music Man Logo, Booth Display

One of our most loyal customers at Music For Everyone, toward the end of the 60's and early 70's was Carl Scroggins. He was a seasoned performer and expert on any thing and everything that had to do with Country Music. He came in one day to buy some strings but mostly to tell us about a new amplifier. He was excited and his voice kicked into high gain. “I mean you can’t believe this darned thinggggggggg!! Cleannnnnnn!! We plugged in a pedal steel and you never heard each one of those chords come through so good! Some friends of Forrest White brought it over to the club for us to try out. They called it a MUSIC MAN!! Carl’s enthusiasm drove the name home, but how could the market squeeze in another amp line? They’d have to go up against Acoustic, Ampeg, Standel, Sunn and even the pretentious CBS Fender, to name a few.

The retail music business has got to be the toughest task in the music industry unless you’re an unlimited funds multi-millionaire. You know there are customers out there somewhere, but how do you locate enough of them to consistently generate a profitable cash flow? Still, retail music is a tremendous education for success in other facets of the industry. By 1974, Jack Steele, my Pacific Music Supply rep, had been named sales manager. Knowing my struggles with retail and failed attempts to satisfy the Cities’ parking requirements in order to build a two story, super-store, he asked me to take over his former sales territory and give ‘reping’ a try. I knew how successful Jack had been. I worked out a satisfactory agreement with my manager, Derek Reymer, to take over my store. A change of business cards, learning to think ‘net’ in stead of ‘list’ and I transposed from retail to wholesale, with out missing a beat!

A five day work week was almost too good to be true. There were no concerns about who is opening or closing, absent personnel, irate customers or unreasonable credit managers. I could schedule my own workday, make friends and sympathize with a long list of Music Store owners, perplexed with the problems I had just put behind me. The next three years flew by. Pacific Music was an ideal employer. May was office manager and credit controller; Jack Steele was sales manager and Bob Rosen, owner. It appeared that I had found a perfect match for my abilities, but change is inevitable.

When Jack called me into his office, I assumed it was the usual sales update. “Frank! You’ve been a good friend and one of my best salesmen. I want you to know how much I’ve appreciated it! I’m leaving Pacific. I’ve been offered a position with Leo Fender’s fantastic new company, MUSIC MAN!!”

There was that name again. I remembered Carl Scroggins excitement when he first blurted out the name, MUSIC MAN! Jack filled me in on some of the details. Leo’s restrictions by CBS were over. He was back in business partnering with Forrest White and Tom Walker. Tom was the Marketing Director for the venture as well as electronics designer of the amplifier division. Tom contacted Jack to be regional sales agent for Southern California, Arizona, New Mexico, West Texas and Hawaii. “This territory is a gold mine,” Jack confided, “I know so many of the Dealers!” We had no idea how soon we’d be working together again!

Several months passed. The phone rang at home. Jack Steele was on the line. “Frank! You’ve got to come down here and talk to Tommy Walker. He needs an accessory manager. This company is the best thing in the industry, the opportunity of a life time!” What could I say? On Saturday morning, September 24th, 1977' I made the 45 minute drive from my Arcadia home to Anaheim, for an interview with Tom Walker at Music Man. The Music Man office and shipping facility was located at 1338 State College Parkway on the corner of Winston Road in Anaheim. The factory was a short walk north. Normally no one would be working on Saturdays. It was a good day for

Tom to come in and concentrate on projects without interruption. When I opened the front door and stepped in to the empty reception area, I could see a light down the hall. Tom's office was big enough to accommodate 5 or 6 visitors comfortably. The executive sized desk fronted a perimeter of shelves and cabinets, some displaying works in progress. Tom was seated at his desk engrossed in paperwork. Sensing my approach, he looked up, smiled, stood, taller than I expected and came over to shake hands. With a Texas flavored greeting, he motioned me to a chair and returned to his desk. We chatted about generalities for 15 or 20 minutes. I noticed that he did not waste words, choosing subjects of common interest discussed intelligently. After a tour of the building, international sales office, domestic sales, accessories inventory and shipping area, we returned to the front entrance. Tom's parting words were essentially, "I'd like you to come to work for us. We need to have our accessory department organized and expanded. I'll need a month or two. You mentioned 30 days notice to Pacific Music Supply. I'll keep that in mind!" I got in my car and headed for the 57 freeway, a lot to think about. I liked Tom Walker. I was impressed by what I'd seen. The starting salary was less than my commissions from Pacific, but future opportunities seemed unlimited and I had evenings and weekends to pursue my other income options.

The Music Man marketing building, 1978, at 1338 State College Parkway, Anaheim, California, 92803. Two years later, we moved to larger quarters, up the street, across from the amp manufacturing complex.

Chapter 2

MUSIC MAN

A Cast of Thousands and their Credits

The fall season, 1977, was a busy one for Pacific Music Supply. All my California accounts, from the northern most in Sonora to the southern most in La Habra, were gearing up for a promising Christmas season. Jack Steele was busy too. I noticed Music Man amps and guitars showing up in his former Pacific Music accounts, most of them presently mine; Pete Jones, Bakersfield; Whittwood, Whittier; Hanich, West Covina and of course, Dick Charles, Glendale; to name a few. December arrived and with it a call from Tom Walker. "Can you stop by Monday the 5th, at 9:00 AM ?" My reply, "I'll be there!" This time the Music Man offices were buzzing like a bee hive. I met Connie, Tom,s secretary and guardian of the reception area. She was totally dedicated to Music Man and would have given her life, if necessary, to defend Tom Walker. Uschi Eastman, head of international sales, besides being a petite, gorgeous, self-reliant German born blonde, was one of the most successful, world-wise sales persons in the music industry. Maureen, her attractive young 'typical American girl' assistant, covered home base with Jenny (South America) and Marti, from France, while Uschi was out of the country.

Don Stouder was the mouth-piece or ear-piece, incoming or out-going, at the order desk, communicating with the U.S. sales force. I would be working with Don, as back up and promoter of Music Man accessories. George Johansson was credit manager, introduced by Tom, as the best in the business. These were the members of the staff I met. Tom gave me a 'start work' date of February 1st , and an invitation to meet the U.S. reps at their annual meeting, Sunday January 15th, the week of the NAMM Show (National Association of Music Merchants), to be held this year at the Disney Land Hotel Convention Center. Christmas season and the 1978 New Year came and went like a dream sequence. I was on my way to Disney Land before I could fully realize a major career change was happening. The upper levels of the hotel over looked billions of dollars of real estate, from mountains to coast line, creating an atmosphere of opulence. By the time I arrived, the two-room suite was humming with conversation between reps, wives and some of Tom's close friends.

Tom Walker was proud of his rep team, "the cream of the crop!" he told me, most of whom had been with him in the original Fender Company: Bud Driver, northern Calif. and the northwest; Tim Driver, Bud's son, the Dakotas to Oklahoma; John Chelchowski, the Chicago area states; Luke Morris and Ron Taylor, East Texas through Florida; Tom Miller, middle east coast; Jody Carver, the phenomenal steel-guitar artist, New York/New England and Jack Steele, So. Calif., Arizona, New Mexico, West Texas and Hawaii.

This group exhibited an atmosphere of success, confidence and invincibility. Tom brought them in a week or so before the show, the red carpet treatment; fine accommodations, plenty of good food and a plethora of camaraderie on the golf course. I left the hotel sorting out names and faces. This was like being called up from double A ball to the big leagues. Would 14 years retail and 4 years wholesale be enough experience to make the team?

Left to right: Tom Walker, Bud Driver, Region 2, Northwest; Jody Carver, Region 8, North East; Luke Morris, Region 5, South East; Tom Miller, Region 6, Mid East; John Chelchowski, Region 7, Great Lakes Central.

Thursday, January 26th, 1978, was my last day with Pacific Music Supply. It came with a surprise party, a cake and some tears. May, Bob Rosen, Kenny and the Staff had become close friends; four years of a positive business relationship. Jack Steele, former sales manager, when he left a year earlier, convinced everyone that Music Man was a career opportunity not to be missed. There was also an unspoken understanding that Pacific Music Supply would be winding up 50 years of music wholesale leadership on the west coast, in a few more years, with retirement of the principals.

On Wednesday morning February 1st, 1978, I drove the 40 plus mile early commute to Music Man in Anaheim, checking in at 7:30 AM, curious to find out what my role would entail? The day was taken up meeting more staff, assignment to a desk, presentation of some classy business cards and instructions on opening and closing the building. Day two in my ledger, a simple entry, 'much to learn'. Day three, ' a scramble to find and count all the items in accessory inventory, staying a couple of hours past closing'!

The second week was high-lighted by an invitation to lunch from Jack Steele, wanting to find out my impression of the companies internal chemistry. Jack was a trumpet player in the legendary Glen Miller Band, a talented performer and arranger. This morning he was on an enthusiastic high, as if he had just played an eight bar riff, an octave above the score! He slapped his Music Man paycheck down on my desk. "This is more money than I deserve! Music Man sells itself!" I didn't have to be a mathematical genius to figure Jack was on his way to a six figure income. He was a dedicated rep, a man of material concerns, optimism and pessimism, strengths and fears. On the long trips through the lonely stretches of Arizona and New Mexico, there was a hand gun beside him in his silver Lincoln Continental. He was one of the 'old school' suit and tie' reps, inflexible, right or wrong. At lunch, we talked about dealers and accessories to complement their Music Man displays. I thanked him for getting me into a career opportunity and a good meal. "We'll do it again!" he volunteered and left to write more business.

Jack's life could have made an interesting biography and motion picture potential. With the Glen Miller Band during World War II, performing for the troops at the front, he survived by being one of the fortunate in the group to fly on a second plane. The first aircraft carrying Glen Miller and the others, was shot down. It was a natural for Jack to go into music sales after the war. Income opportunity for the big bands dwindled, as transportation costs and the rise of small groups, was more suited to night club entertainment budgets. Jack migrated to the West coast where recording activity flourished and took the Pacific Music position for supplementary income. He believed that the Music Man gig would be his last, a crowning performance, leading up to a secure, happy retirement. Unfortunately, an unpredictable Father Time, rearranged the final score!

On February 15th, 1978, my 11th day at Music Man, Tom Walker called me into his office. "I want you to meet Leo Fender! We'll have lunch with him. He probably knows more about electric guitar strings than any one in the industry!" This was a day I will always remember. On the way to lunch I asked Tom why CLF, Leo's factory in Fullerton and Music Man in Anaheim weren't all under one roof? Tom chuckled, a smile spreading across his usually serious face, "it's better that there's plenty of neutral ground between us!" In time I would learn how deep their differences ran. One thing that was obvious, a lunch hosted by Tom was usually at Charlie Brown's or some other up-scale restaurant, This lunch, set up by Leo, one of his regular spots, was the original Carl's Jr., at Carl Karcher Headquarters, 1200 Harbor Blvd., Fullerton, California.

In 1978, Carl's Jr., was more like today's Denny's with a regular full menu as opposed to a fast food counter and drive-thru. Leo was accompanied by his closest friend and right hand man, George Fullerton, both of them products of the same localized country upbringing, They sat on one side of the booth, Tom and I on the other. Handshake introductions preceded relaxed and congenial conversation. Leo asked about my background in the music business, but apparently had already been filled in by Tom or Jack Steele. We eventually got around to talking about guitar strings. Somewhere between a spoonful of soup and a bite of sandwich, Leo said, "get your strings from O.B. Holcomb at GHS. Their quality control is the best of the lot. You'll never go wrong with GHS!!".

As we were leaving, Leo made my day with his parting words, "come by and see me any time I can be helpful!" His recommendation of GHS prefaced an association with the company fundamental to the rest of my music business future. Over the next two weeks, I spent part of each day putting together ideas for a major Music Man guitar string program. My other duties involved inventory control, telephone back up and order processing. Tom's policy for all of us was reassuring. "Open or closed, my office door is always open to anyone of you who has a question!". I regarded this as a unique privilege and most often waited til after hours when only a few of us were finishing up. As it worked out, Tom and I were usually leaving after the others; last one locks up!

The first addition to our string program, which Uschi had capably initiated, was a single gauge string box, for replacement of individual strings, electric or acoustic, .007 through.056. She had set up the MEAM Company in New York to print string envelopes in attention getting orange. These were sent to GHS for stuffing and consolidating into sets to fill purchase orders from Gabe, our factory purchasing agent. Uschi probably had been coached by Leo, although Tom's history with Ernie Ball was a ready source of information, having witnessed Ernie's revolutionizing the guitar string business with his 'Slinky' strings concept. Before Ernie had his own winding machines, in the early days very expensive equipment, he had to have a bulk supplier for the girls in the back of his store, coiling and packaging, for delivery. That first source was GHS, which also could have prompted Uschi's original direction.

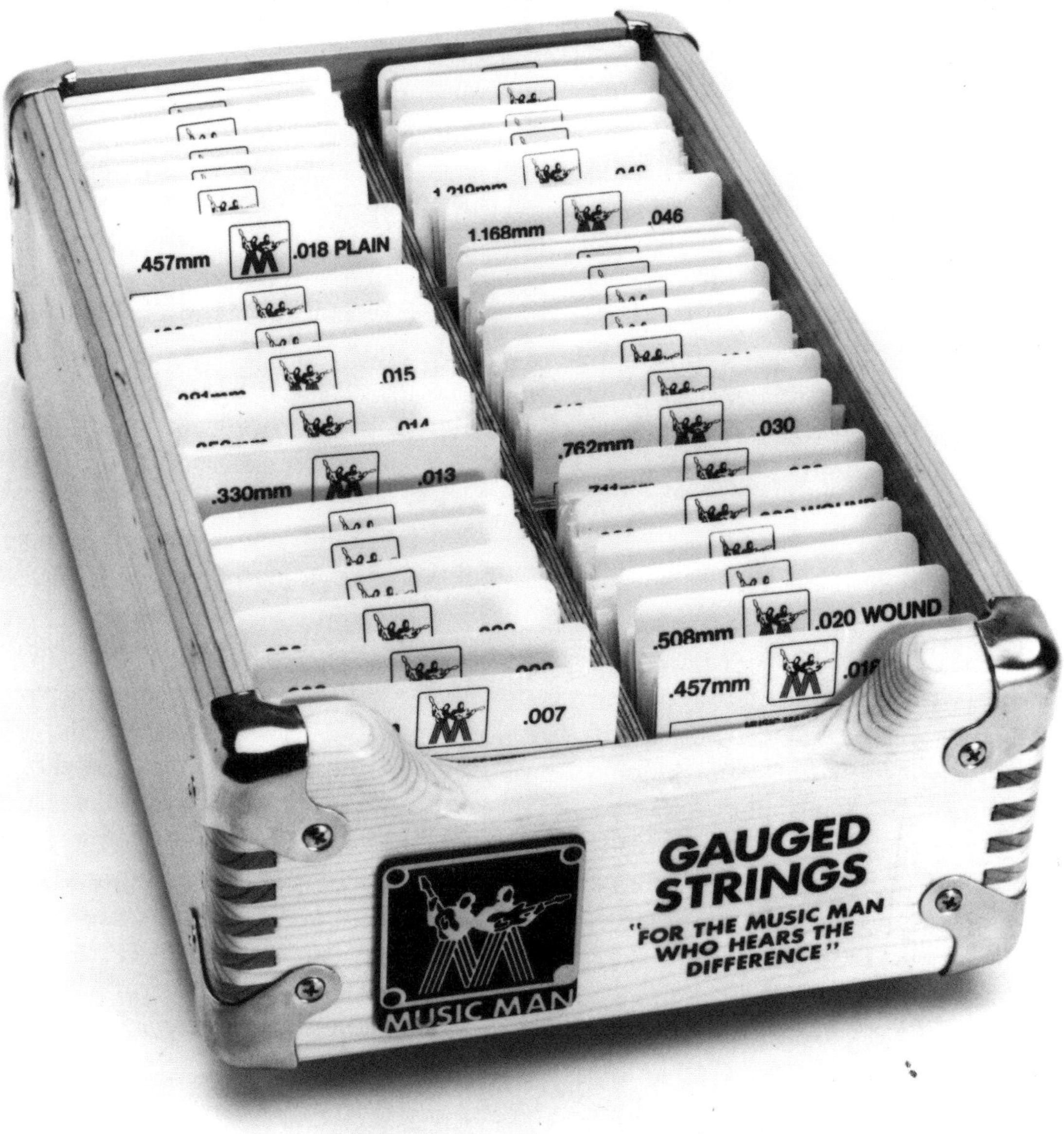

Babe Simoni's state-of-the-art gauge string box built to last 100 years!

I gave Tom a rough drawing of the gauged string box. He approved the project. "We can build anything like that in our woodshop. Go up and see Babe Simoni!" Virgilio 'Babe' Simoni was the menacing gentle giant who ruled the Music Man manufacturing facility at the end of the street, a separate kingdom, worlds apart from the sales oriented marketing office. My first impression of Babe was, "I hope I never have a disagreement with this guy. He could probably neutralize a pack of grizzly bears!", but once Babe smiled and opened up his generous heart, a new friendship began with a wonderful, constructive human being!

Babe was a role model of honest, productive hard work. Starting employment with the Fender Company at age 13, sweeping floors, he learned step by step, every phase of the amp and guitar manufacturing process. He was an iron man, a 'Lou Gehrig' of consecutive appearances on the team, passing up vacations, coming in early, 30 minute lunch breaks at his work bench, staying late when a project needed to be finished and Saturdays when called upon. On top of this dedication, for years he never complained about what could be considered a minimum, minimum wage! Babe tells a story. "I was hired at the factory. One day I was asked to deliver a load of equipment to the main office. There was a lot of bulk, but I figured I could do it in one trip and save time. I had trouble shifting around to get through the office door. A short guy dodged around me, and said, 'you should have done that in two shifts. It would have been much easier!' Babe, young and brash, responded, 'If you can do the job better, do it!!'. When Babe got back to the factory they asked him if he had any problem. 'Only some jerk who thought he could do the job better!" You may have guessed it; Babe's first encounter with Leo Fender! Asked about it later, Leo's comment, "I thought he had spirit and self confidence; good potential!!"

Leo became aware of Babe's developing skills, eventually over-riding the factory supervisor and raising Babe's pay commensurate with the older, but less productive workers on the line. Babe did special projects after hours for Leo, cabinets for the girls in the office and a huge solid chopping block for Leo's special friend, Alvino Rey, to underscore the flexibility of his extra-curricular assignments. This was long before Music Man was even a future fantasy.

The third player was yet to arrive on the scene. One day a young man showed up at the Fender front office, in a plaid suit and cap, applying for work. Leo sent him out on the line to learn amp cabinet covering. A week late, Leo asked Babe, "What do you think of this guy?" Babe's answer, "He's working at it!". Another week passed and Leo asked again. Babe, unabashed, "You want an honest answer. He's never going to be good at covering cabinets, but I don't think that's why you hired him, is it?" Leo paused, "He's got some good ideas about factory management. I wanted to see if he could stick with a hard day's work!". The name of that dapper young man was Forrest White! Thus started a successful career with the original Fender Company and friendship with Leo, that tragically ended with a bitter power struggle in years to come at Music Man.

I don't recall exactly when I met Forrest, the third character in the Leo Fender, Tom Walker triangle that got the Music Man Company off the ground. By the time I signed on, Forrest had been pressed into inactive status and only came down to the office when some monies accrued or a business matter required his signature. Passing by my desk, he stopped, turned on an ear to ear smile and offered his patent greeting for first-timers, "Hi there Buddy, you're new here?". Even after a year or two, I was still 'Buddy'. When he found out I wrote songs, he began bringing me copies of lyrics he had written. Forrest wanted to be recognized as part of Music Man, even though he no longer had active responsibilities.

In retrospect, it is difficult to see how these three men ever came to an original agreement.

Forest White

They were so very different. I liked them all for their good points. Leo was Leo, fast becoming a legend in the guitar industry. He was one of a kind, sometimes friendly, sometimes distant, a dawn to dark pursuer of self-determined goals. Tom was a great boss, turning us loose to create our own successes in the company and anticipating good results. He too, was a tireless worker, a creative electrical engineer, decision maker of design options, of what was then the finest guitar/bass amplifier line on the planet. Forrest was a congenial acquaintance, but the word was out, a some-times tyrannical task master as factory manager.

What separated Tom from the other two, included a sense of direction. If the three of them had booked passage on a time machine headed into the future, Leo and Forrest would have seated themselves in the caboose looking back into the past. Tom would have been up front at the controls, steering toward new trends and possibilities. At the onset, the tremendous potential of the Music Man Company must have numbed them to their differences and convinced them that personality problems would be resolved by the success of the venture. In my humble opinion, had Tom Walker been given a free hand to run the company, Music Man amplifiers would still be the leaders in musician polls today.

Forrest had every opportunity to succeed as factory manager of the Music Man amplifier division. The manufacturing facility he laid out was funded to his requirements. As production began to flow, the new line of amplifiers was clearly an example of excellent quality control. However, there was a growing factory morale problem. Forrest developed a tendency of 'finding faults' as a means of maintaining control and then a policy of 'factory workers' should be 'seen and not heard', bordering on class distinction.

Originally, Leo told Babe Simoni that he wanted him to come over to the guitar factory in Fullerton when it was up and running. Since the amplifiers were the first project, Babe started there, soon demonstrating ability to work every phase of production. Forrest counted heavily on Babe's expertise in spite of their open differences in handling personnel. Another factor was salary. When Babe asked about what he would make going back to CLF, he was told, "go to the superintendent of production, he'll work out a deal for you." There the answer was, 'I'll have to check with the main office." When all was said and done, the offer was not a step up from his situation at Music Man. Babe explains, "Why should I have gone over there and straightened their procedures out, if I wasn't going to make more money?" Changes resolving at Music Man proved he made the right decision. They went at it head to head some times with 'whys or why nots', but always with a mutual goal, the perfect product.

Once Babe got production rolling, the manufacturing facility was the smoothest running division in the Music Man operation. If marketing and Leo's guitar factory, CLF, could have worked together as efficiently, Music Man in its first conception would have prospered and be an industry leader today.

A number of the people at the factory had originally worked for Leo and a few others had friends at marketing down the street. Complaints of Forrest's managing tactics eventually reached Leo and Tom. One of the loudest had to do with the NAMM Show. Forrest told the workers they could not get passes to the show and wouldn't be welcome at the Music Man display, which was specifically for the marketing elite and company executives. Leo was not pleased with implied class distinction. Tom's opinion was in their defense, "they built the product, they're proud of their workmanship, they should be entitled to visit the show and get credit for their performance!" He countermanded Forrest's directive and arranged for their passes.

20 years after their 'gauged string box' project at Music Man, Frank Green and Babe Simoni get together at Babe's office in Anaheim, CA., to design another string box for a Working Musician promotion.

Tensions at the factory continued to grow. Finally Leo and Tom agreed that a change must be made. Stocks were adjusted and Forrest became an inactive partner. He was deeply offended, knowing he had distanced his relationship with Leo, who at one time, Forrest claimed, to be Leo's best friend. The fragile professional respect between Forrest and Tom was now one of disrespect.

Carlos Vasquez, also working on the W/M promo, gets an earful of Music Man history along with a tour of Babe's woodshop and warehouse.

Who could emerge from the ranks, restore factory morale and effectively manage production? If the label 'unanimous approval' ever applied to an appointment, this was the occasion! Virgilio 'Babe' Simoni, long overdue for a leadership role, a gentleman who instinctively down-played his abilities, was at last in the right place at the right time. If the Music Man factory had been a baseball team, Babe would have won the pennant and the world series. He had the respect and affection of both factory and marketing.

I often saw Babe, early in the day, coming down the side walk from the factory and disappearing into Tom'.s office. Shortly after he would be headed back. By mid-afternoon he would return with a proto-type chassis, panel or related component, for Tom's approval.

Not with the intention to leave Forrest White a totally negative figure, it should be remembered that he had many friends. His original association with Leo gave him the opportunity to meet hundreds of Fender enthusiasts and cultivate their admiration. To this day interviews and articles in the trade magazines turn up Forrest White fans. He enjoyed showing up at musical events, visiting music stores and talking to people about vintage amps and guitars. He was knowledgeable and a natural conversationalist.

Randy Hewitson owns Musicians Outlet, a major music store in Palm Desert, California, an upper class destination in the Palm Springs resort area. One day he noticed a mature, sportily dressed gentleman, studying the Fender guitar display at the back of the store. There were others at the counter ahead of him. " I'll be with you in a minute!", Randy called out. Finishing up with a customer, he approached the gentleman. "Is there one of these guitars I can show you?". His reply, "What do you think of the Fender instruments they're building today?"

Left to right; Randy Hewitson, Todd Hudulik, Rob Martinez

Their conversation continued, Randy, being a very knowledgeable player/retailer/collector and this new customer a Fender follower, shared opinions about quality and value of the line dating back to the first strats, tele's, broadcasters and 'P' basses. The visit concluded with a handshake and explanation by the visitor. "I've got to pickup my wife, She's shopping at the mall. I'd like to stop in again, next time I'm down here. "My name's Forrest White!"

Busy with the store, Randy didn't pay particular attention to the name and might have forgotten the incident if he hadn't received a phone call a few days later. "Randy! This is Forrest White. Will you be in tomorrow afternoon?"

In choosing a retirement area, Forrest and his wife selected Sun Lakes, a popular senior citizens community in the San Gorgonio Pass, an hours drive from his former residence in Fullerton, birth place of the Fender Company. Thirty minutes east of Sun Lakes, a down hill descent to Palm Springs, is a wife's shopping paradise. Like most husbands, Forrest's interests were in other things, in his case a music store was a welcome retreat. Finding Randy's Musicians Outlet was just what he needed. He became a regular visitor, on occasion taking Randy to lunch. When Forrest mentioned, "Leo Fender was my best friend!", Randy finally realized who he was. Apparently Forrest's visits were at the time he was writing his autobiography and he wanted people to know about his part in the Fender legend. He brought Randy pictures, articles and even schematics of original amps under his supervision. He gave him copies of songs he wrote and offered him collectibles at reasonable prices, including a 'White' amplifier, Leo built to honor his service to the company. Over the period of Forrest's visits, Randy observed, "he always seemed to be in good health! I was stunned to hear when he passed away! I remember him as a kind and gentle person whose only complaint in life was the failure of Fender to assign valid serial numbers to their early instruments!"

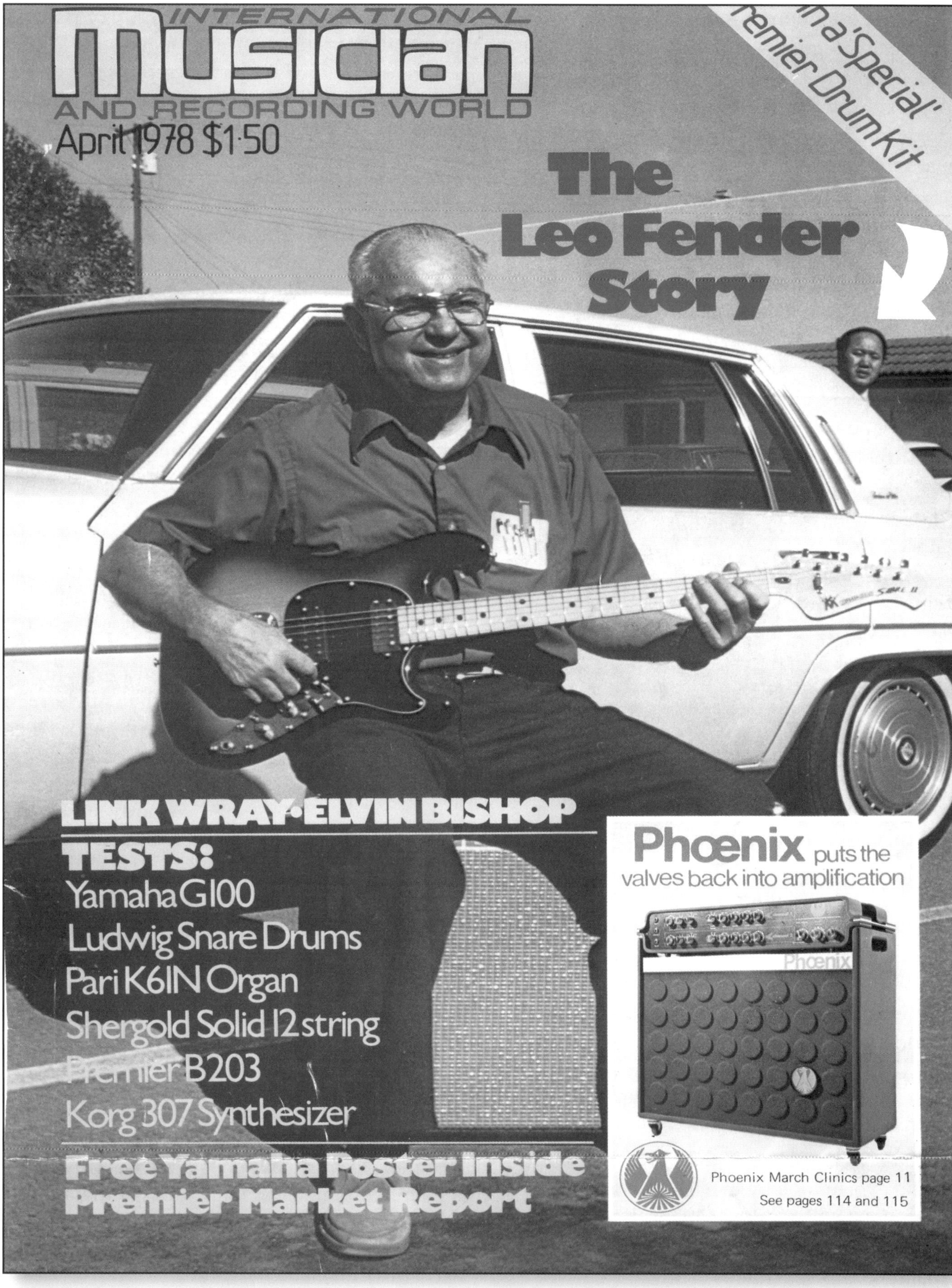

International Magazine, April 1978, Leo with Music Man guitar (being watched!)

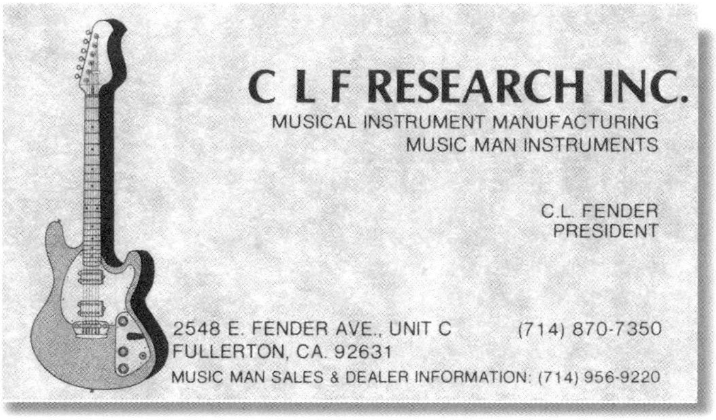

C L F RESEARCH INC.
MUSICAL INSTRUMENT MANUFACTURING
MUSIC MAN INSTRUMENTS

C.L. FENDER
PRESIDENT

2548 E. FENDER AVE., UNIT C (714) 870-7350
FULLERTON, CA. 92631
MUSIC MAN SALES & DEALER INFORMATION: (714) 956-9220

Music Man accessories, built to last!! On September 19th, 2001, I stopped by to see Tim Cartwright, heir to historic PETE JONES MUSIC in Bakersfield, California. Tim, a naturally talented guitarist, began lessons at Pete's store and upon his graduation from highschool, started his own teaching schedule in an upstairs studio. Soon he was working counter sales and playing with Pete on local gigs, a close relationship, paralleling a 'father-son' partnership. Tim explains, "Tom Walker and Music- Man meant a great deal to us, a loyal friend with a superior product!"

Tim poses behind two of the Music Man gauged string boxes.

Frank Green and Tim Cartwright next the Music Man strap rack, 22 years after they were put in service, still as good as new.

The 'gauged string box' project took off in style. Babe quickly had the model built. It was spectacular, an obvious offspring of a Music Man amp cabinet; box joints, polished metal corners and a glossy finish over parallel wood grain. When Babe showed it to Tom, he said, "I can keep the cost down by getting a sticker label for the front." Tom's reply," Use the same logo we put on the amps. Don't worry about the cost. These gauge string boxes represent Music Man quality!"

Another feature that I wanted to include, was heavy-duty, unbendable plastic, gauge cards, dividing the strings in the box and printed with 'set' references for easy customer/clerk broken string replacement. Tom was agreeable and we ordered them in 'Uschi orange', for a strong visual contrast. Twenty years later, as an independent rep visiting music stores, these gauge string boxes and divider cards are still in service, where other brands have self-destructed. With the expected increase in string sales, the responsibility of projecting those increases and ordering the strings came to me. I was given the GHS phone number in Battle Creek, Michigan and told to contact Dave Holcomb, sales manager. This would prove to be a lifetime friendship and the catalyst of my 'after' Music Man reping career. Dave was heir to the 'H' in GHS; Gould, Holcomb and Selko. Dave's father, O.B.Holcomb and mother had been the principals, prior to their retirement and the purchase of GHS by present owners, Bob and Shirley McFee.

Every Music Man Dealer was encouraged to stock Music Man strings, factory installed on all of our guitars and basses. It was a good selling point to tell customers to replace broken or 'tired, strings with their originals. At that time, strings were a profitable accessory for all concerned; manufacturer, distributor, rep and music store, but any new brand had to compete with the market dominance and public perception of established favorites; Ernie Ball, Fender, Gibson, Black Diamond and Guild.

Leo's guitar factory, about five miles north, at the Fender avenue complex in Fullerton, was too close for paying a professional freight carrier. The guitars were brought down to Music Man, in black tolex rectangular cases, vertically stacked in a company pickup truck. Later it was determined that these cases exposed to sunshine or higher temperatures, would melt the plush liner bonding glue, blurring guitar finishes and pitting plated hardware. At first, these instruments were not closely checked, but shipped directly from our warehouse with corresponding amplifier orders nationally and internationally. The early model Stingray I and II guitars, featured different neck radii, (rounder/flatter). It seemed as if these instruments were rushed through to catch up with the already established amp program. The guitars looked and felt, heavy and 'rough hewn'! Their reviews were mixed, but Leo's magical involvement' biased most critics. The Stingray Bass, on the other hand, rose to #1 on world wide polls, in spite of dead spots high on the neck. One enthusiastic retailer commented, "So what! Our market is mainly one-four-five players who never get out of first position!" This was not good enough for the Pro's or Tom Walker. Some tried to blame the problem on string windings, others on neck angle. It became obvious that each bass must be closely checked, re-strung if necessary and neck adjustments made. Shipping often had to be delayed; a very costly inconvenience when overseas containers were dropped off, crowding the loading area and increasing cartage fees. .

By early March of 1978, the guitar deliveries were not matching up with the shipping orders. It fell to my responsibility to design inventory forms to control order flow and a defective guitar procedure. I set up an appointment for March 23rd, with Leo, George Fullerton and Lloyd Chewning to go over to CLF and put together a mutually beneficial approach for guitar ordering and delivery. My purchase order proposal would be based on orders shipped over the last 30 days, plus orders in house, including a colors and models breakdown. Returns, I mentioned, hopefully, would be few.

My meetings at CLF were always positive and in good spirit. Leo and George were aware of my loyalty to Tom Walker, but they also knew of my genuine friendship toward them. How much we accomplished that day, is hard to say. We avoided disagreements and concentrated on the order projections. They accepted their copies and thanked me for bringing them over. As a parting message for Tom, they wanted to assure him, "quality control has always been a CLF priority!"

Meanwhile the accessory program continued to flourish. We ordered light weight three ring black binders with a gold Music Man logo on the front, for the growing list of accessory items; all the string gauges, straps, shirts and displays, easily accessible for dealer counter reference. One of the 'perks' of company involvement are the incentives offered by suppliers. Tom frowned on any of us accepting them, which I was unaware of at the time. Gabe and Barry up at manufacturing had their own set of rules; got free tickets to an Angel ball game and invited me to come along. Angel Stadium was just down the road. We spent a great evening; Angels 5, Toronto, 4. Projects for May included a visit to the Victoria Case Company in Los Angeles to discuss options we could offer through the accessory catalog. June, an opportunity to have lunch with bassist, Carole Kaye and delivery of a Sabre Bass for her endorsement. When Tom was out of the office on other business and Jack Steele or Uschi couldn't cover, I was 'back up'! They all wanted to see Tom, but I made a lot of friends.

June 24-27 were the dates for Summer NAMM, still the big show and still in Chicago. Tom and the rep staff would man the booth and unveil the latest gear. Music Man's unique hybrid amps, combining solid state and tube innovations, were the talk of the industry. A deluge of orders came in from the show and the rest of the summer was taken up building and shipping product. Tom's vacation started on Monday, August 28th. We held the fort until his return on September 12th. The fall season saw momentum gathering, Babe's amplifier team turning out flawless product in increasing numbers. Guitars and basses were coming in, but more and more, couldn't pass inspection and had to be returned to CLF. Still, December 1st, proved to be the biggest shipping day of the year. Spirits were high! The annual Music Man Christmas party included a turkey and a box of See's Candy for everyone up the street at manufacturing, as well as the staff here at marketing. If that wasn't enough, a four day holiday to follow.

How unpredictable life is! When I was so deeply involved in retail music in the 60's, I never would have guessed I would be at Music Man in 1978! Merry Christmas everyone!!

January 1, 1979, page 12 catalog

Chapter 3

MUSIC MAN

Music Man is #1; All Systems Go!!

Wednesday, January 3rd, 1979, the new year starts off on a positive note. My desk has been moved to a spacious, quieter area. Right away, business picked up where it left off, all products moving well. On January 25th. We started setting up for the NAMM Show, this coming weekend, again at The Disneyland Convention Center. The reps came in early for their week of golf. I believe Tom looked forward to these get-togethers on the links as much as anyone, he himself, a proficient golfer. The show was upbeat and generated a lot more orders. The gauge string boxes and the new bass string box drew many compliments. Traffic at the booth was consistent and the visitors enthusiastic. The show was over too quickly and cleanup afterwards seemed to be the longest part of the event.

February 1st, marked one whole year at Music Man for me. I took Gabe, the factory purchasing agent to lunch at the Silver Fox restaurant. He would be leaving Music Man shortly for an upgrade opportunity. He was a non-musician, so the music part of a job was not important to him. He was very helpful to me in getting my accessory sources set up and I wanted to show my appreciation. On the 29th, Tom left for the Frankfurt Music Fair, the largest music trade show in the world, for some years to come, until NAMM moved it's offices from Chicago to Carlsbad, California; bringing a winter trade show to Southern California Convention Centers and eventually challenging Frankfurt for top billing. Uschi had established Music Man as an International presence in the amp and guitar world. Containers for Europe regularly left our dock, amps with voltage adjustments for the particular country and guitars and basses still not problem free. One shipment of guitars and basses arrived in Northern Europe with fractured finishes. An unstable paint formula was blamed for the failure and the entire order had to be written off. In spite off the instrument set-backs, confidence in Music Man produced a strong order response from Frankfurt. Combined with a growing domestic market and a $150,000 container to Japan, Friday March 23rd, 1979, was the biggest month to date in Music Man's relatively short existence.

The future looked fantastic! Music Man was #1 in the polls of the most popular music groups around the world. All the sales force and Babe's manufacturing crew, saw a clear path to career fulfillment. There was only one oversight in the game plan and that was the inconsistency of CLF quality control. The tremendous success of the Music Man venture and the almost unlimited potential of a Music Man/CLF team, could not bridge the widening gap of personal differences. To the neutral knowledgeable, up-to-date observer, Music Man was on the right track. If CLF could have recognized the trends of the times and taken a follow-the-leader roll, nothing would have stopped them. Music Man, the brand name, evolving with new designs and products yet unknown, would still be headquartered in the Fullerton/Anaheim locations of it's origin.

Music Man set up it's own QC (quality control) to try and prevent any defective guitars or basses being shipped. Jeff, Jotty and Steve were very intelligent and talented guitar players, who felt they were three of the luckiest guys on the planet, to be able to play Music Man instruments all day long. There was no hurry, no pressure, just play the guitars and basses. There were critique sheets to fill out, with a final signed verdict; pass or reject. Some things they couldn't determine easily; reaction of the finish to other climates or internal truss rod complications.

The bigger the instrument orders became, the higher the level of rejects. Someone at Clf started the rumor that, "They are returning guitars and basses that are perfectly saleable. We're the experts! They're just 'hot-shot' kids. Keep the returns a week or two and send 'em back again!" This was a bad mistake! Jeff, Jotty and Steve were all experienced in custom setups. Once they found dead spots, high frets, bad harmonics, intermittent electronics or any of the multitude of problems that can plague an instrument, they noted them on their critique sheets and subconsciously recalled them from having spent playing time with the instrument. Many of their reports read, "this guitar was checked previously and the same problem exists!"

Tom and Leo came to an impasse where they could no longer discuss issues face to face. Their basic philosophies were light years apart. CLF felt Music Man spent too much on image; Music Man, that CLF spent too little. We had carpeted floors and central air conditioning. They had linoleum and rattling window mounted units. Both Tom and Leo were perfectionists to their own perceptions. Several of us in marketing were the 'go-betweens'. We felt Tom was right in his approach to present and immediate future music industry survival, but we didn't want to tarnish the public's hero image of Leo Fender, 'father of the electric guitar'! My personal belief was that CLF could never catch up with Music Man's tremendously successful head start in production. CLF was not ready to mass produce guitars and basses. Also, their workers were paid on piecework. The more each one could turn out, the more he'd be paid. CLF believed their past credits justified present products, whether or not the professional musician of the day agreed. CLF quality control was biased. In their hurry to fill orders and be reimbursed, they were ineffective, to say the least. The problem compounded their production. They couldn't build more without moving what they had, including returns. Someone spread the word that Music Man was refusing product to put CLF out of business. This made no sense. Music Man was back-ordered and desperately needed guitars and basses to complete orders and satisfy dealers.

Toward the end of May, Leo was asked to look at the new Peavey guitars. I was recruited to pick up samples from Dick Charles Music, in Glendale, one of the most successful music stores in California. The chance to visit Dick, one of Jack Steele's best friends and spend a 'neutral' afternoon with Leo, was a welcome opportunity. Watching and listening to Leo analyze an instrument is an education. In this instance, he wasn't impressed with the sample guitars, nor did he think young Hartley Peavey had much of a chance to make it in the music industry. In later years Hartley took satisfaction proving the 'old men' were wrong!

Monday May 14th, Dan Hoy came to Music Man as Traffic Manager, to help solve warehouse problems. The staging area had to be in the parking lot. Every evening pallets of product were fork-lifted back inside the building into cramped aisles and every morning the process was reversed to allow access to the rest of the inventory.

Dan was up to the task, always cheerful, never complaining about coming in early or staying late to maintain control. Greg DeLorto, a talented Christian guitarist, was brought in to assist Dan with paperwork and procedures.

Tom felt that more personnel were justified by the companies rapid growth. Jill and Jane were added to Connie's secretarial staff to deal with increasing correspondence and receptionist coverage at the entry desk. Three more, important recruits, would complete the roster.

One evening after closing time, two of us left in the building, Tom was in a rare talkative mood. "Roger Balmer is a young executive over at Yamaha. I've been watching him for some time. He may be the answer to our communication problems with CLF. Roger has agreed to come over to us after his present agreement ends this month".

Roger proved to be a very likeable person. A shirt and tie dresser, he always looked managerial. For the first eight weeks he listened and analyzed each one of our jobs. With Tom, he visited CLF and again, listened and studied their operation. Next to arrive was Mark Wentling, a brilliant young engineer/performer with a background in design and manufacture of effect pedals and amplifier options, popular with 'cool' musicians of the day. Tom and Mark became very close friends; Tom as much of a 'father figure' as an employer, which Mark recalls with deep appreciation.

Uschi's decision earlier in the year, to start her own company, E and E Exports, left a vacuum in the overseas division. She was such a successful and seasoned veteran in her field, that her replacement was difficult; particularly so, considering Leo's respect for her. She couldn't change his thinking, but she could bend his direction on occasion. He was often speechless in her presence and valued her friendship.

Both Tom and Leo liked blondes! Not to be deterred, Tom went to a reputable employment agency and found another one. Enter Elisabeth Pedraza! Besides being attractive, she was German born and educated with considerable sales experience in other fields. She had much to learn about a new and unfamiliar product line, as well as overcoming small talk; "She'll never be another Uschi!" My answer was, "give her some time and you'll say, 'there'll never be another Elisabeth'"!

I gave her all the support I could. When she found out I had never been to Europe, she insisted, "You've got to come to the Frankfurt Music Trade Show next spring!" She was right. I started planning and applied for a passport several days later.

Elisabeth Pedraza on the phone, Jenny, Marti, and Maureen smile at the camera. The Music Man Export Division was one of the best in the industry.

On July 23rd, 1979, Mark Wentling joined the R&D team at Music Man taking on a portion of Tom's work load; the beginning of a mutual friendship that enriched both of their lives. Mark recalls his first days: "When I arrived I began working with Barry Klein and Dave Lacy, who together made up the R&D team with Tom. Tom had his own lab adjacent to his office, where he would conceptualize and breadboard the amplifier designs. Barry and Dave would assist in the fabrication chores and perform some debugging. Dave was an accomplished guitarist who had played the Las Vegas circuit. Barry was a keen experimenter with a strong interest in solid state effects. Barry came to Music Man through Leo Fender, who was a family friend.. Tom, being a ham radio buff, was the tube guru. He also collaborated wit Leo and a tech named Bob Luly on the very first amp designs.

The R&D Team in the Lab. Left to right; Dave Lacy, Barry Klein and Mark.

The new building was occupied in January 1980

With Tom's confidence in Elisabeth (and as I mentioned, Leo likes blondes,) Music Man moved forward without skipping a beat. Roger Balmer had all of us under assignment, Mark Wentling relieved Tom of many technical projects and Babe Simoni directed amp production as finely tuned as the Boston Symphony.

One of Roger Balmer's first directives to me, was to upgrade the string packaging. 'Uschi orange' didn't fit his criteria for a strong marketing impact. His concept was something that stands out in a music store's wall string display with metallic gold print. I relished this kind of creative challenge and started to work immediately.

Making a phone call to Dave Holcomb at GHS to let him in on our packaging changes, he told me he would be coming to California the following week. "Could we have lunch?" My enthusiastic 'yes' emphasized the chance to meet Dave face to face. Over the last year, along with string orders on the phone, we had also shared common interests, tennis being one. Years later when I visited him in Michigan, he had switched to ping-pong. I heard he was a local champ!

On Tuesday, October 16th, 1979, Dave arrived at Music Man. He was a perfect match to his phone personality; full of good humor, an abundance of energy and extremely knowledgeable about strings and fretted instruments. We toured the marketing facility, went up the street to the amp factory, then out to lunch. The day cemented a friendship that over the next 20+ years high-lighted Music Trade Shows, visits to GHS, performances of his banjo mastery and an autographed copy of his first book:

'Raining Cats And Doggerel!'

Roger Balmer's first assignments to the accessory department, was a new string packaging. He felt Uschi's original "orange" did not project a strong enough marketing impact.

It was important that the Music Man logo be visable among competing brands on a Music Store's wall display. Bright colors with metallic gold print was the answer.

Dave Holcomb,
V.P. Sales GHS Corporation
(And Banjo Virtuoso!!)

The new string labels meant locating a printer that could work with gold leaf weight stock. My friend Bill McCartin in Glendora, who had done our 3-ring plastic binders for dealer accessory cataloging, was enlisted to print samples for guitar and bass string packaging. Dave would have GHS ship product without labels. We would stuff the new ones on arrival. More accessory items were added to our stock. In particular, Silver Eagle nylon straps with Music Man logos, to complement our basic inventory of 21/2" and 31/2" custom leathers from John Keckler.

November and the extra day after Thanksgiving arrived before we could catch our breath. Business was increasing faster than we could make room for it. Talk of a larger facility filtered around, but where? Tom announced a Christmas party for Friday December 21st, preceding a company vacation until December 26th, when we would start our move out of 1338 to the cavernous complex at the end of the cul-de-sac, directly across from manufacturing. Babe's daily walks to consult with Tom were reduced to a hop, skip and a jump! By the 29th, we were in. All the principals, including myself, had private offices. Roger Balmer's office had room for staff meetings with stained wooden cabinets along two walls. He brought in his huge back log of Music Industry Trade Magazines and almost filled the cabinets. He subscribed to every publication related to the music business. Rumor had it he sat up in bed til after midnight several times a week digesting every word. He had an exceptional capacity to absorb information and wanted to be conversant on every facet of our involvement in the industry.

I was given expanded space in the warehouse to accommodate my growing accessory inventory. Every new idea crossing my mind, to be built in manufacturing by Babe Simoni, like the string boxes, floor standing strap racks and counter displays; or ordered from outside sources such as golf shirts, pick boxes and polish products, etc., had to be OK'd by Tom. He never said no! I questioned him about it. "That's what I hired you for," he said, "as long as Music Man keeps growing, we can afford to!" Then prophetically, "If we stop, things can turn around awfully fast!"At the close of 1979, barring the problems with CLF, this was the farthest thing from my mind!

Don Stouder, our very popular, in-house phone contact for the Sales Reps and their accounts, takes a week end hike, free from phones and order blanks, on the slopes of Mt. San Jacinto, looking down on sun-baked Palm Springs.

Leo and Esther, his first wife, on their yacht, 1972; One of Leo's best years!

Chapter 4

1980, New Office/Warehouse/Catalog

As we came to work on Wednesday morning January 2nd, 1980, in our newly refurbished head-quarters, there was a strong sense of pride in Music Man. Preparations for the up-coming Western NAMM Show, (National Association of Music Merchants) at Disneyland on Friday January 18th, introduced a 'state of the art' Music Man products catalog (see page 68), eventually to become a 'collectable', prized by players and musical equipment 'history buffs' around the world.

Tom Walker's opening preface, in the Catalog on page 4, highlights Music Man's beginnings, purpose and goals. Page 5, pictures 30 flags of countries supporting and distributing Music Man instruments. There's a wealth of amp and guitar information, plus excellent photography on the succeeding pages. Also, don't miss page 44, my department, accessories! (The 44 still prevailsonmy email,greenman44@verizon.net).The NAMM Shows; West Coast, Chicago/East and Frankfurt,Germany, were positive spring-boards for Music Man. Tom always brought the sales team in early for the Anaheim dates, to visit the home office, preview new products and as mentioned in an earlier chapter, to play golf! On Tuesday January 15th, they arrived. Work came to a halt, as greetings and personal updates were exchanged.

Thousands of attendees at the NAMM Shows including Music Store owners, their employees and associates, pack the aisles to see new products from manufacturers and distributors; national and international, name brands and first timers.

On Friday morning there was a large crowd waiting outside the hall to get an early look at the displays. The rep team, suited up in a 'which one of us looks best' fashion statement, eagerly watched for customers from their own territories. Jack Steele and Bud Driver would have the advantage from their California, Nevada and Arizona dealers. The first day was always well attended by International groups, flying in advance for week long accommodations. The traditional NAMM member marching band opened the show. Music Man was soon swarming with potential buyers. The RD Series (Reverb/Distortion), foot-switchable control, was most appealing to young 'rockers'.

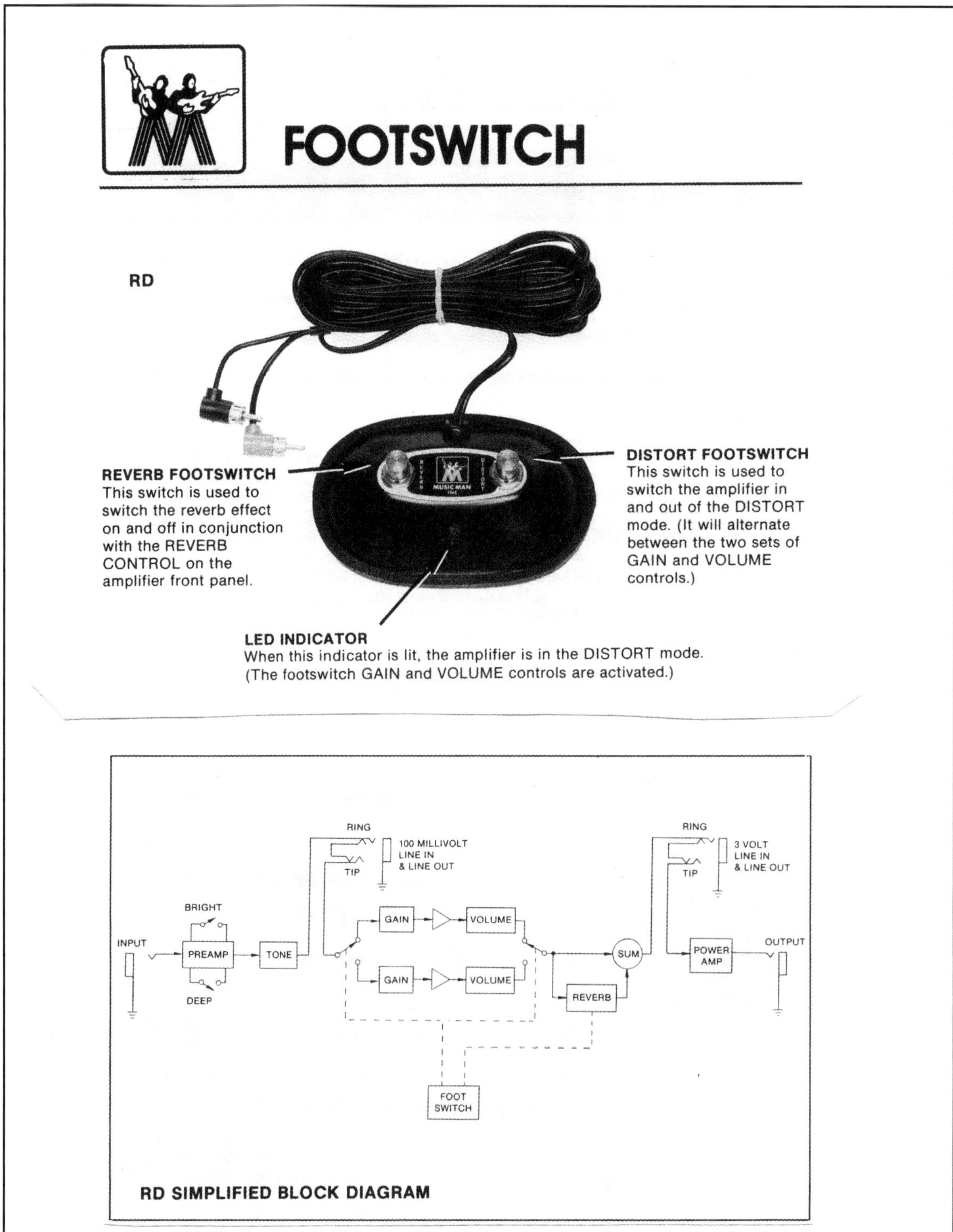

Interest in the guitars and basses paralleled the amps. The problem our Music Man quality control guys faced, was finding instruments that would meet Music man standards. The growing pile of rejects headed back to CLF, some being returned for the second and third times, reduced saleable inventory alarmingly. Basses were by far the biggest attraction among the instruments. The Stingray Bass, when it was right, was the envy of the industry and the newer Sabre model creating a viable option for the player.

The Anaheim Show featured an endurance contest not widely publicized. Three key figures were Pete Jones, of Pete Jones Music in Bakersfield, California; Jack Steele, Music Man rep; Tom Walker and anyone else who would care to join them. Which one would be the last one to leave their annual late evening bar party and first to show up at the booth next morning? It was pretty much of a draw between the three. They were all veterans of midnight toasting and disciplined early morning rising.

Momentum from the show carried over on Monday. Music Man's popularity in Japan had created a tourist destination. A big high-rider tour bus pulled up in front. A stream of Japanese, camera carrying vacationers converged on our building. Their English was limited, but they could say 'Music Man'! They took pictures of everything and everybody, then went across to the factory and repeated the process. Their friendly exuberance and product loyalty was appreciated.

February 1st, was just around the corner. All efforts focused on the Frankfurt Show at the end of the month. My own plans to attend must be put into action. Dean Brown, one of my closest friends, former celebrated high-school band director, now a music store owner, was to make the trip with me. Dean knew Europe better than many people know their home state. Mention a trip to him and he would say, "when are we leaving?" I wanted him to meet Elisabeth and scheduled a luncheon for February 5th, at a restaurant nearby Music Man. We arrived in separate vehicles; Elisabeth in her bright yellow convertible Volkswagon beatle. Sometimes with the top down and her grammar school aged daughter along, she looked like an older sister on their way to the beach,

Elisabeth and Dean hit it off immediately, sharing favorite destinations in Germany, France, Switzerland and Austria. She would arrange an evening for us after show hours in Frankfurt. Dean had already set up our itinerary; flight, accommodations and some sight seeing. The rest of the day back at Music Man involved the shipments for Frankfurt; my concern, the accessory displays.

On the 15th, Tom, Roger and Elisabeth left for Europe to supervise setting up the booth and meeting room. Contacts with key dealers and appointments to be verified would make profitable use of pre-show time. The following Thursday, I drove down to Music Man to finish up odds and ends, transfer daily responsibilities to Don Stouder and check in with Babe Simoni at the factory for last minute input to Tom. Friday morning at home; final packing, did I forget anything? Goodbyes to family, pickup Dean and head for the outside extended stay parking at LAX. Take the shuttle to west terminal and wait in line for boarding passes on Condor Airlines Boeing 707.

Taking off over the blue pacific into a setting sun sinking over the edge of the ocean, was inspiring. Circling back over Orange County, Music Man somewhere below in the sprinkling of early evening lights, Mt. Wilson coming up, towering above my Arcadia home at the base; I tried to put in perspective what the Music Man experience had done for me. From a small music store owner in Sierra Madre, California, to local territory reping for Pacific Music Supply, to a position at Music Man with contacts all over the U.S.A. and now Europe.

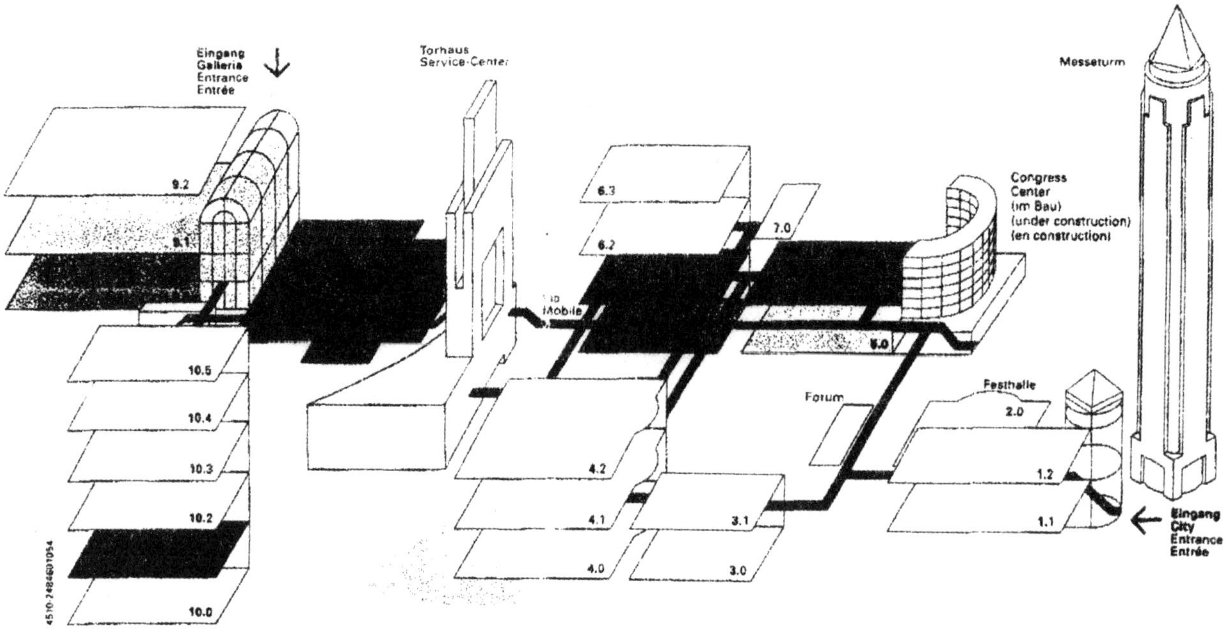

The world's Number One Trade Fair shows you the way forward.

The Hall plan, the "who is where" of the music fair will help you to find your way around without problems. And the "Via Mobile" connects the halls so you can reach them easily and quickly. There is also a shuttle bus between the halls. The individual product groups are to be found in the following hall levels:

Hall 5.0
Rock-Pop Stage, Lasershows

Hall 5.1
Sound & Audio Equipment, Sound Recording Studio Equipment, Accessories

Hall 6.0
Lighting & Special Effects

Hall 6.1
Sound & Audio Equipment, Sound Recording Studio Equipment, Accessories

Hall 8.0
Stringed Instruments, Woodwind & Brass Instruments, Percussion Instruments, Sheet Music, Accessories

Hall 9.0
Electronic Keyboard Instruments, Electronic Church Organs, Computers, Hard- and Software, Accessories

Hall 9.1
Electric Guitars & Basses, Amplifiers & Accessories

Hall 10.1
Piano Salon: Pianos, Grand Pianos, Historic Keyboard Instruments, Pipe Organs, Accessories

Galleria
Stage for Traditional Musical Instruments

Frankfurt Fair complex

Music Man had given me credentials for a life time career in the Music Industry. A fuel stop in Chicago and 12 more hours over the Atlantic brought us into Frankfurt. A passport check at customs and the purchase of Eurail passes set the stage for our agenda. Dean's planning was first class!

Our reservation in the castle at St. Goar, featured a spectacular view high above the Rhine River. Living on a pinnacle is a royal privilege, but tough if you forgot to pickup a quart of milk!

In the morning we eurailed to Frankfurt and checked in at the Hotel Rex, our residence during the show. Approaching the Fairplex is unforgettable; it's huge, maybe a square mile in circumference. .Even though the music event was the largest of its kind at that time, only a corner of the grounds housed some 1500 displays for the 80,000 visitors. A five day schedule was divided; the first three exclusive to Music Industry members; the last two, open to the public. At the 1980 exhibit, a shuttle bus took you to the various music halls. Our booth was in the electric guitar, bass and amplifier hall. Acoustic instruments had a separate location. You couldn't miss the over sized logo identifying Music Man.

An impressive selection of guitars and basses was fronted by stair-step risers lined with amplifiers and speaker cabinets. The accessory display of upgraded packaging was sure to attract attention. The draped, sound enclosed meeting room in back, was where Tom hung out for specific appointments. Otherwise he was gone with any number of friends or for necessary business meetings. Roger Balmer had his own following generated in part by his previous employment with Yamaha. Elisabeth was in her element, fluent in local and neighboring languages, she was never without a potential buyer. Seeing Dean, she excused herself to present him with tickets for a special show sponsored, opera night. She had noted his love of classical music. The Frankfurt Fair, unlike its American counterpart, drowning in 'Rock', devotes a major portion of promotions to the Classics. I stayed at the booth to assist with accessory customers while Dean went off to look at band instruments. I cautioned him, "don't buy anything until you have at least 24 hours to think about it!" Dean's store was over stocked after every trade show. He loved to pick up new products, but often suffered later figuring out how to pay for them. After the show closed, we hurried back to the hotel to dress up in opera attire. Elisabeth's tickets were 3rd row center, for a magnificent performance of 'Don Giovanni'.

Day two of the fair was another busy one. Tom, Roger and Elisabeth had all they could handle, so I met with some of the overflow. An Italian group and another from Holland, both speaking good English, occupied my morning. Later in the day, a gentleman with a line of microphones, asked to see the Accessory Manager and gave me catalogs and price lists. I told him no decision could be made today. I would contact him after I returned to Anaheim. Dinner that evening was at Sachenhaus, one of Dean's favorites when in Frankfurt. The morning of the third day, Dean and I checked out of the Rex. Today would be our last at the show. Days four and five were open to the public. Everything in the booth was 'battened down' to survive the human tidal wave of 'want-to-be's' and 'freebie' seekers. All net prices and 'dealer confidential' materials were removed. Some local distributor assistance could be recruited to greet musician referrals from the area. Tom would have many other things to attend. I was excused early in the afternoon. Dean was close by. We went straight to the rail station, Eurail passes in hand.

The following week encompassed a loop through Amsterdam, Paris, Switzerland,

FRANKFURT - THE INTERNATIONAL MUSIC TRADE FAIR

The International Music Trades, the grandest of music goods fairs
In a complex full of cubicles laid out in little squares,
Where the universal language is music to the ears,
of retailers, distributors and all their financeers,
who deal in pianos, guitars and sheet music,
Accordions, percussion and strings,
Woodwinds, brasses, endless accessories
And all the electronic things.
At the end of the day when the trading is done,
The camaraderie grows.
As the spirit of Frankfurt warms the night,
Where the beer and the afelsaft flows.

DEAN

TRAIN RIDE THROUGH THE ALPS

From Zurich, to Innsbruch, to Zell Am Zee (zay),
Past lakes and mountains on a snowy white day,
With dining car and compartment first class,
You can live like a king on a Eurail pass.

FRANK

EURAILPASS 1¢

15 days — first day / last day

Mr Green
Country ______ Passport No. ______

This ticket is strictly personal and not transferable

KLEINBUSSE MIRABELLPLATZ
PANORAMA BUS TOURS

Mirabellplatz - Andrakirche, Telefon 06222/74029

TICKET 01313 *
Sound of Music
includes City and Lake Tour

price: As 160.- depart: 9.30 a.m.

Dean and Frank at the Frankfurt Fair

Vienna and Southern Germany; returning to the Frankfurt Airport for a 747 flight over Greenland and the Polar Icecap back to LAX. I spent time on the trains and in the air writing down accounts of the trip, interlaced with a few poems. Thank you Music Man for an introduction to Europe!

Back to work at Music Man, there was a backlog of work to catch up. The export ladies were hard at it processing orders from a number of different countries. Roger wanted an up-to-date guitar/bass projection, by model and color, based on shipments the last 30 days, inventory in stock and unfilled orders in house. Once these figures were compiled, the procedure was to call CLF an make an appointment to bring them over, usually the next day. Sometimes I'd meet with Lloyd Chewning, Production Manager, or George Fullerton, or Leo himself. After a major event like Frankfurt, it would be all three! Even though the gap between Music Man and CLF was widening daily, I never had a problem arranging a meeting. They knew I liked them individually and had no axe to grind collectively. They realized I was a company man totally loyal to Tom Walker, but answered questions honestly; some they didn't want to ask Tom or Roger directly.

Before they looked at the order projections, they wanted to know all about Frankfurt. Was it really well attended? Did the key accounts come to the booth? What did they say regarding the guitars and basses? Were there problems with any of the amps? Lastly, how was Elisabeth Pedraza received? I was really pleased to tell them she was a smash hit! When we got around to the guitar/bass purchase orders, the tough questions came up. "We can't continue to build instruments for you with so many rejects. Are your men told to return half of what we send you to keep our profits down? I didn't want to get into the changing of the times, when early Fender instruments were shipped directly to stores, pulled out of the box and hung on the wall. Kids coming in would buy anything that said Fender on it. Most of them were one, four, five players and just happy to have a name brand instrument. Major setups were done for more professional customers and serious problems fell under warranty repair.

The market today was far more sophisticated, buyers were educated and most important the large container shipments to foreign distributors. Problems with wood and finishes were increased under the conditions of a long sea voyage and what could they do if the instruments were landed unsaleable? I avoided getting in to this area and answered from my observation of the receiving step by step procedure. "Our QC guys are on their own. They treat each instrument as if they were going to buy it. They're pro-players, who have worked on guitar set-ups at local music stores. They fill out a report on each one; finish, play-ability up and down the neck, intonation and electronics. If they pass it, it's shipped, if not they request a return!"

I was aware of the thinking at CLF, that these young QC checkers should come to them to learn from their years of experience what makes a saleable instrument. In Roger Balmer's case, he too was a 'youngster' in their eyes and Yamaha as a background, related to the 'Asian invasion'; looking over Leo's shoulder for his next move in the Music Industry. The guitar cases which came with the instruments from CLF were found to be the cause of blurred finishes and rust pitted hardware. The animal glue used to hold the plush case lining, had a low melting temperature and dripped through on the instrument.

Windows in my office looked out on the hood of my Ford Escort wagon parked directly in front. I took a damaged case with a trashed guitar inside and put it on top of the hood exposed to direct sunlight. After

JW.
Given to Leo on 3/26 per our phone conversation

TO LEO BAD QC MAR 24 80.P

MUSIC MAN, INC.
1338 State College Parkway
P.O. Box 4589
Anaheim, California 92803
(714) 956-9220
Telex 692-397

March 24, 1980

Mr. Leo Fender
CLF RESEARCH
2548 E. Fender Ave., Unit C
Fullerton, CA 92631

Dear Leo:

This letter is written to alert you of increasing quality control problems that have been encountered over the past six to eight weeks. Lloyd, of course, is aware of these problems and has been very helpful in taking steps to correct them. It is important that these problems be corrected now before they reach a "crisis" stage.

Our instrument reject rate has increased from 8% in January (which is the lowest percentage of rejects since we began our quality control program) to 28.8% in February to well over 60% so far this month. The rate of repairs at CLF has not kept pace with this increase, resulting in a reject inventory at Music Man totaling 116 instruments as of Friday. Our records indicate a reject inventory at CLF of 18 instruments, bringing the Friday total to 134 rejects.

The increased time required for inspection and documentation, plus the increase in the number of instruments to be tested, has caused our only quality control technician to fall behind in testing -- resulting in an untested inventory of 155 units. It is probable that most of these instruments will be subject to the same high reject rate we have experienced so far this month.

In addition, two entire shipments totaling about 80 instruments have been returned from our distributor in the Netherlands for CREDIT due to extreme quality control problems. A partial inspection of the first returned shipment reveals severe neck and finish defects. These continuted problems have caused our distributor to stop importing Music Man instruments until he is assured they have been resolved.

After successful strong efforts by CLF and Music Man late last year to bring the reject inventory of about 500 units down to zero and strong improvements in quality control and quality control standards, there remains a lack of consistency in maintaining the desired quality control level. It is imperative that strong efforts be made at CLF to restore quality control and reduce reject inventory in process to no more than 10 - 15% of weekly production.

It is imperative that immediate efforts be made by both CLF and Music Man to reduce our reject and untested inventory to zero within the next <u>two weeks</u> so that commitments to our dealers and distributors can be fulfilled in April.

A detailed list of problems is attached, along with a recap of February's reject rate. The March rate will be available on Tuesday.

As you know, it is my personal strong belief that there is great potential for expansion of Music Man instrument sales in the near future provided the proper steps are taken to update our existing products, develop a variety of new products and adhere to our quality control standards. We can expect to make no further progress in the market unless progress is made to bring our quality control up to standard.

Yours truly,

MUSIC MAN, INC.

Roger Balmer

RB/cg

encl: a/s

WEEK 6-13		BODY/NECK PROJECTION																					SPECIFY: RIGHT HAND	YES	OR: LEFT HAND	NO
DATE: 3/24/80		STINGRAY BASS BODIES							SABRE BASS BODIES																	
DATE	WEEK	B	N	S/T	S/B	W/L	W/H	TOTAL	B	N	S/T	S/B	W/L	W/H	TOTAL	B	N	S/T	S/B	W/L	W/H	TOTAL	COMMENTS			
INV. →		0	0	0	0	0	0	0	0	0	0	0	0	0	0							0				
4/28	6	8	14	3	12	3	3	43	10	12	3	11	6	5	47							90				
5/5	7	8	14	3	12	3	3	43	10	12	3	11	6	5	[illegible]							90				
5/12	8	8	14	3	12	3	3	43	10	12	3	[illegible]	6	5	[illegible]							90				
5/19	9	8	14	3	12	3	3	43	10	12	3	[illegible]	6	5	[illegible]							90				
5/26	10	8	14	3	12	3	3	43	10	12	3	[illegible]	6	5	[illegible]							90				
6/2	11	8	14	3	12	3	3	43	10	12	3	[illegible]	6	5	[illegible]							90				
6/9	12	8	14	3	12	3	3	43	10	12	3	[illegible]	6	5	[illegible]							90				
6/16	13	8	14	3	12	3	3	43	10	12	3	[illegible]	6	5	[illegible]							90				
TOTALS		64	112	24	96	24	24	344	[illegible]	[illegible]	24	[illegible]	48	[illegible]	376							720				720

DATE	WEEK	STANDARD BASS NECK: MAPLE W/FRET	STANDARD BASS NECK: ROSEWOOD W/FRET	STANDARD BASS NECK: EBONY F/LESS	NARROW BASS NECK: MAPLE W/FRET	NARROW BASS NECK: ROSEWOOD W/FRET	NARROW BASS NECK: EBONY F/LESS	TOTAL
INV. →		0	0	0	0	0	0	0
4/28	6	28	28	7	14	10	3	90
5/5	7	28	28	7	14	10	3	90
5/12	8	28	28	7	14	10	3	90
5/19	9	28	28	7	14	10	3	90
5/26	10	25	31	7	14	10	3	90
6/2	11	25	31	7	14	10	3	90
6/9	12	25	31	7	14	10	3	90
6/16	13	25	31	7	14	10	3	90

MUSIC MAN, INC.

7/7/80

FRK TO RGR REPAIRS JUL7 80.PDF

MEMO: Roger Balmer

FROM: Frank

SUBJECT: C.L.F. REPAIRS

I received a call from Lloyd this morning expressing concern and frustration on 2nd and 3rd time repairs.

His conclusion was that C.L.F. will not continue to do 2nd and 3rd repairs where they feel they have adequately repaired the instruments, as shown on the service request, the first time around.

He contends that they fix what is on the service request and the instrument is returned again for correction of yet another problem. He states that "Sean" does most all final inspection and is well-qualified to determine the satisfactory completion of the work.

Sean and Steve obviously disagree on "quality control" standards.

Steve lists several current discrepancies!

1. Truss-rod nut loose; rod rattling even when nut is tight.
2. Action not set to "specs" and cannot be set to "specs" without string rattle.
3. Truss-rod adjustment effective only between 1st and 14th to 16th fret.
4. All sabre guitars cut too wide in nut grooves with resultant string buzz.
5. String spacing still bad at nut.
6. Finish on sides tends to "orange peel" and have scratches.

Lloyd has agreed to meet with Steve and myself at 10:00 A.M. 7/8/80 to personally examine these problems along with the current repairs at C.L.F.

lunch, I brought the case in and opened it. The guitar was spattered with small drops of a sticky brown substance. I showed Tom and Roger, then called CLF for permission to contact the case company. I drove into L.A. with test case and guitar. The factory was helpful and started immediately to correct the problem. They had already experienced some complaints from UPS making deliveries to California desert areas where dealers held them responsible for temperature control in their vehicles. The case factory also understood my concern for container shipments, on deck, in transit overseas. In the meantime, we looked at other sources, including air mold cases.

On May 22nd, Music Man had a visit from Matteis Meyer, son and heir of Gottholdt Meyer, the largest Music Man distributor in Germany and long time personal friend of Tom Walker. Rumor had it, that beside business, Matteis came to see Elisabeth, whose exceptional performance in Frankfurt caught his attention and a growing friendship resulted; the beginning of a permanent relationship. June was occupied with preparations for Summer NAMM in Chicago. Originally, Chicago was the big U.S. Show, with emphasis on stocking up for a successful fall rental and Christmas season. By 1989, thinking changed. January NAMM on the west coast and planning for the whole year, became necessary. Jack Steele dreaded the summer show; said it was the worst time to be in Chicago when humidity levels were unbearable. Never the less, business was good. The new accessory floor-standing strap rack, with amp corners, wood-burned Music Man logo and black plastic hangers; a Babe Simoni work of art, generated a flurry of strap orders along with the usual popularity of amps and guitars..

July 11th and another Music Man visit by Matteis Meyer included Elisabeth's invitation to be their guest at El Torrito for lunch. I enjoyed their company; a well matched entertaining couple. Later in the month, Don Stouder took his annual vacation, putting me in the 'hot seat'; fielding phone orders from reps and dealers. If I didn't already appreciate Don's daily contribution to Music Man's performance, I was further convinced. The phone never stopped from 9:00 AM to 5:00PM. August arrived before any one noticed. Another project Roger handed me was to schedule a potential US amp production for the next 30 days. Export took care of their requirements. The situation facing both of us was the shortage of tubes fundamental to the Music Man sound. Tom had developed a unique circuitry for pro-longed tube life, which further increased the demand for amplifiers. But, if you can't get tubes, you're in trouble. The industry, beyond musical products, was headed in another direction, solid state and other power sources.

Our back-orders for units we couldn't build until the shortage was rectified, posed a question. What can we come up with to keep the factory working? Speaker cabinets were doable, but even certain models of speakers were slow delivery. I wrestled with last month's shipment record, orders in house and probable parts arrivals until 9:00 PM that night. I knew Roger would want some paper work in the morning. I thought about the man at the top who had to pay the bills; Tom Walker. I never heard him complain, outside of an occasional observation of human nature!

September, in the accessory department, concentrated on Super Screen printed items from their factory in Long Beach. Give-a-way tote bags, so popular at the trade shows; golf shirts and 'T' shirts, profitable inventory, were consistent repeat orders.

October gave me an opportunity to visit local music stores and get their input on our Music Man accessory program. Valley Arts Music, just over the hill from the Sunset Strip, was one of the most respected and successful independent music merchants in the Western U.S.

RD SERIES

AMPLIFIER SPECIFICATIONS

		RD Series	RP Series
POWER OUTPUT DELIVERED TO 4 OR 8 OHM SPEAKERS		ALL — 100 models, 100 watts RMS ALL — 65 models, 65 watts RMS	
INDIVIDUAL MODELS (Followed by speaker quantity, type, and nominal diameter, except as noted for head-only models)		RD-100 (Head)	RP-100 (Head)
		112-RD65 1 Music Man 12″	112-RP65 1 Music Man 12″
		112-RD 100-EVM 1 EVM 12″	112-RP 100-EVM 1 EVM 12″
		115-RD 100-EVM 1 EVM 15″	115-RP 100-EVM 1 EVM 15″
		210-RD 100 2 Music Man 10″	210-RP 100 2 Music Man 10″
MINIMUM INPUT SENSITIVITY	Input 1 Input 2	1 mV 2 mV	1 mV 2 mV
INPUT IMPEDANCE	Input 1 Input 2	215K ohms 122K ohms	215K ohms 122K ohms
TONE CONTROL CENTER FREQUENCIES	Treble Middle Bass	3.3 kHz 460 Hz 65 Hz	3.3 kHz 460 Hz 65 Hz
BRIGHT SWITCH BOOST		+12 dB @3.2 kHz	+12 dB @3.2 kHz
DEEP SWITCH BOOST		+13 dB @54 Hz	+13 dB @54 Hz
LOW LEVEL LINE IN/OUT JACK	Nom. Level Output Z Input Z	0.1 volts RMS < 700 ohms > 180K ohms	0.1 volts RMS < 700 ohms > 180K ohms
HIGH LEVEL LINE IN/OUT JACK	Nom. Level Output Z Input Z	3 volts RMS < 700 ohms > 180K ohms	3 volts RMS < 700 ohms > 180K ohms
PHASER RATE		Not Applicable	0.05 Hz - 8 Hz
REVERB		Footswitchable	Footswitchable
POWER REQUIREMENTS ±		120 V AC, 60 Hz	120 V AC, 60 Hz
3 AG FUSE RATING		3 amp	3 amp
NOTES:		2 Gain & 2 Volume controls, footswitch selectable	Footswitchable 4 stage phaser

TUBE REPLACEMENT — Due to the many circuit refinements found in your MUSIC MAN amplifier, the vacuum tubes should run cooler and longer than in most other high power amplifiers. In the event that a tube does fail or become noisy, it should only be replaced with a tube of the same type number. The tube type numbers are listed in the tube location diagram located inside the wooden cabinet. Matched tube pairs are not necessary, but it is good practice to replace the full set in the event of any tube failure as this will help assure a longer time before subsequent replacement. Depending on use and handling, some tubes can last as long as several years.

Most of the pro's and recording musicians in North Hollywood and up along Ventura Blvd., traded there. The repair shop was well qualified and a warranty station for leading brands. Their full time luthier creation, Valley Arts acoustic guitars, were second to none in construction and quality. Valley Arts was a strong Music Man Dealer, one of Jack Steele's key accounts. He was pleased when he found out they had given me a large accessory order. Another in Jack's territory, Derek Dammer's store, with the unlikely name of Nadine's, was right in the center of Hollywood's hotly contested retail music scene. Derek was an aggressive Music Man promoter and made sure our equipment was in the hands of musicians at popular clubs and recording studios. Nadine's eventually expanded to a valley location and Derek's favorite vacation site, a third store in Hawaii. He liked anything that had a Music Man logo on it: displays, strings, straps, picks, cables, casters, cases, bags, golf shirts. 'T' shirts; he ordered them all!

The end of October and daylight saving time, for me, meant the 45 mile drive home after dark, not a problem, but something to consider; moving my residence to the Anaheim area. Changes were going on all around the world. Tuesday morning I stopped by the firehouse, local polling place, to vote, then drove on to Music Man. It was evening before I had a chance to turn on the radio; "KFI 640 reports, a media polls check predicts a Ronald Reagan victory!"

The World was in for a big change! Music Man shifted to high gear. Back orders on tubes and speakers were catching up. Dan Hoy's crew was busy loading over seas containers, UPS and inter-state freight-liners.

The Thanksgiving break was a welcome interlude; much to be grateful! December proved to be a race against time, to cap off the biggest year in Music Man history, with every possible sales effort. We worked up until the morning of the 24th; the last half day reserved for the annual Christmas party! Cheers everyone! So much for 1980!!

Chapter 5

MUSIC MAN

1981, The Plot Thickens! A Nation Divided Against Itself!

Untimely scheduling of the NAMM Show and Frankfurt, made January a pressure cooker of preparations. The Disneyland Hotel could no longer contains the Show's growth. Over flow from the previous year had to be set up along the driveway entrance to under ground parking. The move across Katella Avenue to the Anaheim Convention Center necessitated acceptance of a Friday, February 6th, starting date, just a few short weeks before the Frankfurt Music Fair. Some companies, who had to ship their displays from one show to another, were faced with the decision of which to attend. Music Man would participate in both, shipping to storage area in Frankfurt before a January NAMM deadline, while benefitting from Ernie Ball's ace construction expert, Dan Norton, creating a Music Man 'attention getting' booth display. The amp, guitar, accessories and promotional shipment for Frankfurt, was completed on January 26th; the Anaheim Show now full speed ahead. Rather than rent carpet from the convention center, the decision to purchase would make sense for future shows in Anaheim; projected as the long term Western NAMM location. What Color? In memory of Uschi, orange!

Pictured below: The new Music Man display; lower left, Mark Wentling, head turned, watches a couple examining literature; Frank Green, three piece suit, prepares to greet a 'white-shoed' prospect; while Bud Driver looks off into the maize of human activity, possibly contemplating lunch!

Music Man accessories displayed well, with the black outline and metallic gold logos. The show's growth in attendance often congested the aisles and sporadically over-crowded the booths. The evening entertainment on Saturday night, featured a country music celebratio. I invited my son Mike and several friends.

February came and went, beginning with Western NAMM and ending with the Music Man principals annual Frankfurt visit. On the surface the new year appeared to be a continuing success story, but rumors of CLF descent filtered through to us. Roger Balmer's attempt to correct the instrument problems backfired. He reasoned that if CLF wouldn't listen to Music Man's findings, they would certainly respond to respected authorities on guitar construction and technical analysis..Roger brought in John Carruthers, columnist for several noted trade publications and designer of the latest approach to building trouble free instruments. John took samples of Music Man guitars and basses, writing an extensive report on how to improve them. His findings were presented to CLF to implement.

Again, CLF rejected criticism of their instruments. Their response was indignation. "These young, 'flash-in-the-pan', so called experts, should come to us for advice. We were building guitars when they were just learning how to play one!" Secretly, at first, CLF conceived the idea of marketing their guitars under another name to prove how well they would be accepted by their old Fender dealers. CLF (Clarence Leo Fender) introduced Gand L (George Fullerton and Leo Fender). They still felt that Music Man was not moving their product in an attempt to gain control of their production. Not so! In fact, Music Man was suffering from not being able to fill orders, satisfy Dealer complaints and maintain needed profitability.

Most all the people at CLF were honest, capable employees. Lloyd Chewning was dedicated, knowledgeable and always helpful. George and Leo couldn't have been more receptive to me personally. Ryan Crampton, who I met in later years and wrote about in my book, 'The Custom Guitar Shop and Wayne Charvel', was one of Leo's best men on the line and went on to many successes, one as IMC's 'Quality Control' manager at the Charvel/Jackson facility in Ontario, California, by the airport.

Somewhere in the CLF procedure there was a 'glitch'. Maybe it was the 'piece work' scramble to get units out. Maybe there was a weak link in the chain. What ever it was, CLF would never admit to 98% of the discrepancies that turned up in their instruments. The general feeling at Music Man was still optimistic. We were part of a major career destiny! In March, my inclination was to find a place close to Music Man. I opened a bank account and looked at real estate offerings. When I told Tom about my decision, for the first time I felt the uncertainty of Music Man's future. Tom paused, a concerned expression on his face, "No, don't leave your present home. I wouldn't want you to be hurt by a situation beyond my control!" I'll never forget his words of consideration, nor did I mention our conversation to anyone. Beneath what some considered a 'stonewall' business attitude, Tom Walker cared deeply for all those who were loyal to him.

I remembered the meeting with Tom late in 1979, when I had remarked on the 'go ahead' purchase orders for new accessory projects and he had said, "As long as Music Man keeps growing we can afford to (OK purchase orders). If we stop (growing), things can turn around awfully fast!" I began to notice changes. There were layoffs. The extras that were brought in to handle growth, were disappearing. I over heard some conversations of difficulty to meet payroll.

Music Man having to assume losses for defective instruments that CLF would not and unable to ship enough guitars and basses to fill orders, had to start looking for other sources. My contacts from past reping for Pacific Music, gave me an interesting update on G&L instruments. Some of the first ones they built had the same neck and intonation problems Music Man experienced. One of my dealer friends in the lower San Joaquin Valley area, was contacted by the new G&L rep to have a sales demonstration at his store. He was asked to invite all the guitar players in the area to critique the new line. Apparently, the rep stopped by G&L on his way north and picked up instruments from the shipping department, but not have time to check them. According to my friend, the event was a total embarrassment. Un-casing the new guitars and tuning them, each one was found to have a problem making it unsaleable. G&L eventually got their act together, but didn't reach it's present respected pro-status until it was acquired by BBE Sound, Inc. of Huntington Beach, California. To G&L's credit, they stuck with it until they became successful.

With amplifier sales stalled for parts and some design changes, a few rep complaints that commissions were down, its understandable why Tom had his hands full. In defense of sales reps in general, I will mention my own experience. A commissioned rep makes a sale. The dealer gets dated billing or runs into tough times. After the dealer eventually pays the distributor, your monthly commission check arrives. I recently received a check for a sale I wrote ten months ago and I'm sure many reps have waited longer.

By June of 1981, wanting to help out where possible, I told Connie, time card keeper, I would volunteer for half day hours, (which meant half pay) over the summer and fall months. I had weekend income at the Palm Springs Tennis Club, playing tennis with prospective timeshare buyers, certainly an enjoyable part-time occupation. I was still able to control the accessory inventory, maintain contact with the reps and visit local music stores to assist Jack Steele and Bud Driver with accessory sales. I no longer had my spacious private office; now a desk with the main group of congenial constant conversationalists. The unpredictable actions of Forrest White, kept them buzzing for some time. I was not there and am not sure of the date. From what I was told, Forrest burst in the front entrance, went straight to Tom's office, opened and slammed the door. The girls could hear him shouting at Tom. There was a loud crash! As Connie got up to see what happened, Forrest charged out, exited quickly and drove off. Tom appeared, unflappable through trial or triumph, holding a guitar neck. " He swung at me, I warded it off and it wiped out everything on the desk!" Forrest had many grudges and grievances! Which one prompted his reaction, I never heard.

The half day schedule demanded good time management to get things done. Imprinted bottles with the Music Man logo, added private label guitar polish to the accessory list. Computerized inventory came to Music Man and SKU labels had to be assigned to all the items in my department. Days and weeks flew by. The annual Music Man Christmas party convened in Tom's office at 2:00 PM , Thursday, December 24th. The spirit was warm! The toasts were many, but the number of faces, fewer than last year.

Moose McMains purchased his
MUSIC MAN SABRE BASS
at Nadine's Music, Hollywood, California!

Chapter 6

1982, Someone Pulled the Plug, Before the GIG was Finished!!

Monday, January 4th, 1982, I returned to a full day Music Man work schedule in preparation for the NAMM Show and anticipating a rebounding year for Music Man. I proposed a program for purchasers of Music Man strings to save the black and gold logo package labels for incentive rewards, thus encouraging more string sales. When I had my music store, it would have worked, but no one else was excited about saving labels. Show preparations were at the top of the list. Another late start for Western NAMM collided with Frankfurt Show dates. Working on both at the same time had some advantages for accessories. One master order could be divided without concern for voltages or container packaging required by amps and instruments. All day Thursday, February 4th, entailed short trips, back and forth, between Music Man and the Anaheim Center, getting ready for Friday's opening. The display looked terrific! The record crowds were enthusiastic! The Future?? The energy from the show carried over into the next week.

NAMM SHOW DISPLAYS

New ideas for accessories flooded my mind. One was an outlandish contraption; a guitar case that opens up into a guitar stand and music rack. A teacher or small club gigster, could set up in limited space with guitar and fake book ready for action. Babe Simoni was very supportive of my ideas and would have built a proto-type, but this one never got off the ground. I wanted to stock enough accessory products to go on commission and relieve Music Man of withholding and hourly wage expense. Accessories could be sold to non-dealers, which our reps would never have time to call on. I had an annual vacation coming up and I planned visits to my former Pacific Music accounts as far north as Southern Oregon. I would bring the results back for Tom to consider. There was also the possibility that I could find new accounts for the reps or strengthen existing ones. As a test, I called Bud Driver and discussed my long time friendship with Sound Stage in Fresno and Fife and Drum in Visalia. We agreed to meet on a Monday morning in Fresno and do product workshops through the day. Bud was very pleased with the results, encouraging me to go ahead with my plans.

The biggest stumbling blocks for Music Man were yet to be over come. As I look back, one in particular, could have been the most debilitating. Kanda Shokai, Japan, was one of our largest most loyal distributors. Our QC guys were very thorough, but what they could not see, slipped by. Excerpts from a Mark Wentling contribution tell the story: "There are actually Music Man instruments that were manufactured by the CLF factory which have straight truss rods in the neck. These necks obviously could never adjust. When tightened they just randomly warp, snap the rod, or even break apart. Kanda Shokai Japan literally replaced hundreds of necks in their stock with Japanese made copies. Music Man issued thousands of dollars in credits for these defective instruments losing all kinds of money.

I still have some of these necks sawed open, which will hopefully make it into a book some day. The really weird thing is that in order to have been made, someone had to change the physical tooling at CLF. To do that would cost money. Its hard to believe that Leo himself would be involved, but how did the tooling change get put through and paid for? If Leo did not know then (somebody) most certainly knew!

Tom Walker had clear grounds for a law suit, but preferred not to. I guess partly because it would be a real negative, publicity wise, and cost wise. Also, Tom being a determined and self sufficient Texan, instead, chose to source necks and bodies from Grover Jackson at Charvel and final assemble instruments in the Anaheim amp factory. Tom had the confidence and determination to make a go of it without CLF. Tom also invested heavily in Geoff Gould's Modulus instrument company developing carbon graphite necks for the Music Man basses. The necks were tough to make, but a good one, mounted properly on a Stingray body was an incredible sounding instrument. Players like Joel D'Bartolo were nuts about them!" Tom had a tough road to hoe. Music Man, at its inception, was Leo, the money man, a 50% stockholder. Tom and Forrest had 25% each. After the manufacturing power struggle came to an impasse, an agreement was reached to give Tom 26% and Forrest 24%, now a silent partner.

The earlier shipment in 1978 had correct curved truss rods. The mystery is, who changed the neck tooling when it was right in the first place? No one at CLF would take the blame! Music Man lost thousands of dollars in time and replacement costs. It appeared that CLF had 'shot itself in the foot', but no one knew, who 'pulled the trigger?'Could someone possibly have thought, "if we straighten out the truss rod, we won't have any more warped or twisted necks? If we tighten a straight rod, the neck will be held in place?"The anonymous 'trigger' man would have to have been new to guitar and bass building, but adept at tool and die design!

Musical Instruments & Accessories

Since 1948

March 25, 1980

Mr. Rodger Balmer
Music Man, Inc.
1338 State College Parkway
Anaheim, CA. 92803 U.S.A.

KANDA SHOKAI NECKS.PDF

Dear Mr. Rodger:

We are doing our very best to sell more Music Man's Products. WE hear the problems from our customers about Bass Guitar's Necks as followed.

Neck adjustment rod does not work perfectly as this bad sample. We tightened the rod as tight as possible, but still the same.

We found those kind of Necks almost 60% both Maple finger-board and Rosewood fingerboard Necks.

You can see the cracks between nut and first fret where the truss rod nut goes in. And after tuned in correct pitch as G, D, A, E, the neck goes bowed very badly.

I cut the one Stingray Bass Neck to see how the rod is in the neck. I thought that the rod is inlayed in the neck as the same way as Catalog's picture.(Page 16-17 at the bottom) But I found it is not. It is inlayed just straight from the nut to the end just angled.

We believe that Catalog's way is very correct. Have you changed this in that way?

We need extra necks which are working good.(Both Stingray and Sabre, Maple and Rosewood Fingerboard, 10 pieces of each.)

And also we would like to know about same neck troubles in the U.S. and other countries.

If you are in a position to do this for me, it will make me very happy.

Very truly yours,

Kanda Shokai Corporation

Takahiro Saitoh

RR# 02700
4-1-80

Kanda Shokai Corporation
4-2. Kandakajicho 3-chome. Chiyodaku. Tokyo 101. Japan
Phone 03/254 3641 Telex:2225269 GRECO J

The letter to Roger Balmer from Takahiro Saitoh of Kando Shokai refers to the bass guitar neck problem illustrated by this photograph. The shipment of February 4th, 1980 arrived with improper straight truss rods.

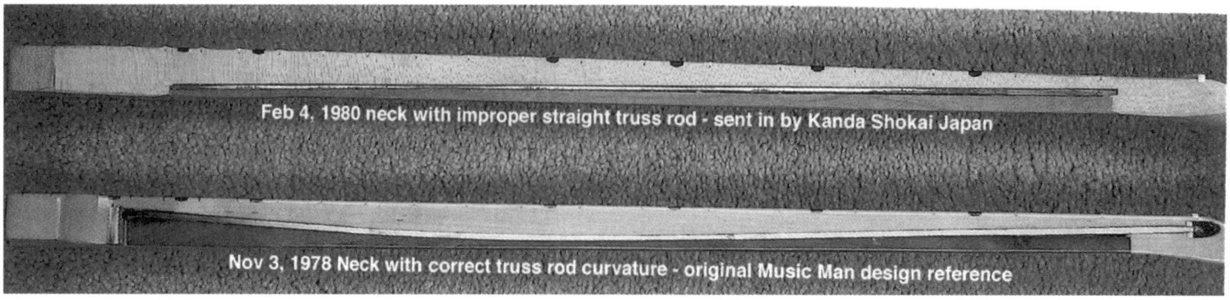

How could Tom make it? A 26% stockholder, without the 50% money man? This didn't dawn on me right away. I was too busy trying to make my own contributions profitable to the company. Strap locks were a new addition and a novel idea, belt buckle covers featuring a Music Man logo. Why should a player scratch up the back of his favorite instrument, when a simple thing like a belt buckle cover could prevent it?

Concentrating on the little things, I didn't tackle the big things. Who would have listened to me anyway? Twenty four years later, writing the finishing chapters of this book, I have the answer. A Monday morning quarterback always knows the play that should have been called.. There was one man who had the confidence of both Leo and Tom. One man who always came to work early, knew everyone's job on the line, stepped in where someone was absent and did their work, to keep production rolling. CLF and Music Man were only about five miles apart. Working the morning shift at one location and after lunch the other, both facilities would have been in harmony, turning out the best products in the industry. They should have tripled his pay!

Babe Simoni would have saved the day! Ernie Ball still could have stepped in later on ; Tom retreating to his quiet home in San Luis Obispo. The amplifiers, like the guitars, to be best in class at the trade shows and Babe Simoni, the gentle giant, recognized for his true genius! As the story, in reality, turned out, Babe probably was better off, at peace with the world, running his own successful wood-working company at 2841 East White Star Lane, Anaheim, California, 92806.

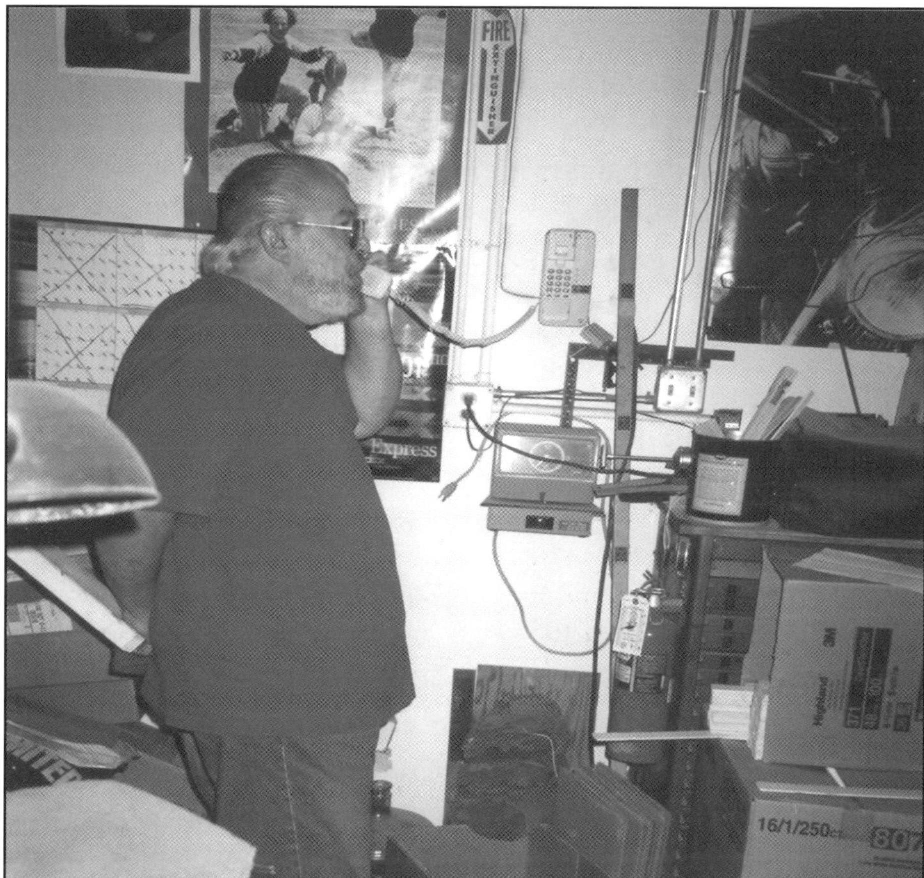

Babe Simoni

Returning to the spring of 1982, I was preparing for my vacation/accessory tour and new additions for summer NAMM. The Music Man endorsement artists were not aware of internal problems. When they were in the area, they often stopped by. Large, hi-rider busses pulled into the parking lot, vivid colors and lettering: 'The Dolly Parden Tour' and 'Alabama' to name a few. Music Man offered automatic equipment updates. The 'roadies' would unload their gear, then pile into the office to see Tom. At the trade shows many of them stopped by and were asked to play the instruments and test the amps. Jim Soldi, past guitarist with the Johnny Cash Band, presently managing the family music store in El Cajon, California, tells of an occasion when Leo was sitting by his side at the booth. Jim was trying out a new Music Man guitar and drew a crowd of appreciative listeners. He recalls, "Leo kept whispering, 'louder! louder!' and would reach over giving my master volume a twist!"

On June 7th, I left for the first leg of my vacation music store tour; the Escort Wagon loaded with Music Man accessories and promotional materials. First stop was Tom's, Jack's and my favorite, Pete Jones Music in Bakersfield. Pete already had every Music Man guitar, amp and accessory in stock, but I couldn't pass up an opportunity for an update. Next visit was Fife and Drum in Visalia; then Sound Stage, Fresno; Venturi in Madera; last, Lewis and Sewell in Merced, for an evening clinic. The following day, up to highway 49, Cole Music in Sonora, on to Charlie Robinson, in Chico and then to Herreid's in Redding. I took a two day stop over in Mt. Shasta, visiting some recreational property I own and reminiscing back to 1955 through 1957, when I gave accordion lessons in the logging towns around the base of the 14,162 foot peak. Off again to Sound Senter Music in Yreka; John's Music, Medford, Oregon; a store in Grant's Pass; then back in California at The Hub, in Crescent City. I planned a full accessory workshop for Maxon's Music in Eureka, one of Bud Driver's established accounts, who would never get a 'hands on' presentation for employees, unless they all made the 600 mile trip south for the NAMM Show. An early departure along the redwood highway, to route #1 cutoff, out by the ocean at Ft. Bragg, for Fiddles and Cameras, Mendocino Music and a remote distributor, Lark In The Morning.

Time was running out, so I by-passed the Bay area, a Bud Driver stronghold and drove to Robbin's Music, in Hollister, for a planned accessory clinic. In the home stretch, now approaching Payne's Music, Paso Robles; Premier, San Luis Obispo; Happy Music and Sousa's in Santa Maria; straight to Arcadia; I arrived late that night. Back at Music Man Tuesday morning, June 15th, I turned in the new dealer accessory applications from the trip. There were new projects to get started, including: guitar cables, road jackets, cordura bass bag material and 'glow-labels' from the Hezik Company. Making up a stock book for a fiscal year end accessory inventory, kept me occupied into July.

On the 29th, the Marshall Crenshaw Band came to town, for an appearance on the Merv Griffin Show in Hollywood. I was elected to deliver speaker cabinets for the performance. The band was very impressive! A positive ending of July, preceded an ominous beginning to August. More layoffs at Music Man signaled major changes. Don Stouder's annual vacation was scheduled to begin Monday the 2nd. He confided in me his feeling that he too, might be terminated. I was surprised to hear that from Don. He was the link at the phone order desk to domestic income formaintaining Music Man's daily operation. From what he implied, I suspected his vacation included researching other opportunities. I was asked to cover the order desk in his absence. The question entered my mind, how much longer will I be here? Busy on the order 'hot-seat', I couldn't dwell on it. Also, new accessory items; Beldon cable with 'heat-shrink' reinforcements, upgrade right- angle plugs and five inch header cards for packaging the cables, kept me active til the end of the month.

Wednesday morning, September 1st, Tom asked me to come into his office. Closing the door, he motioned me to a chair in front of his desk. With a solemn face, his words were something to this effect. "Music Man is facing cash flow problems! Do you have other employment options?" Recent events prepared me for this to some degree. "I'm versatile," I contrived, "and my exposure here at Music Man has opened a world of contacts. I'm grateful for the experience!" Tom seemed relieved! We talked about the direction of the music industry. I concluded the conversation. "I can clean up all my projects by next Tuesday and transfer accessory purchasing to Babe's office." 'You don't have to!" Tom volunteered. I wanted to let him know I was concerned for Music Man. "I still have strong friendships here. I want to be sure the accessory program continues. I'll stay in touch!" We shook hands. I went back to my desk, cleaned everything out and took purchasing files up to Babe. I believe he already knew. He felt badly about it. "I'll be around for another week finishing up!" Another handshake, a giant one!

Winding down my Music Man projects, entailed a visit to Customline Design for new bass string labels, while keeping the door open to what I might do in the future. The same approach to my other suppliers, completed the week. The Labor Day long weekend with family and Tennis Club business in Palm Springs was a busy one. Tuesday morning September 7th, 1982, I made the last drive down the 57 Freeway to Anaheim as a Music Man employee. Connie had a generous check for me, followed by more handshakes and some hugs. On the way home, I decided to stop at CLF and break the news. The secretary called Leo. He came up front with some of the others. I suspect they were already aware, but acted surprised. Leo's last words, "I'm sorry to see you leave, but I don't want to break off communications!" Several times later, he called me. For the next six weeks, I sorted things out, asking myself,

"WHAT'S NEXT??

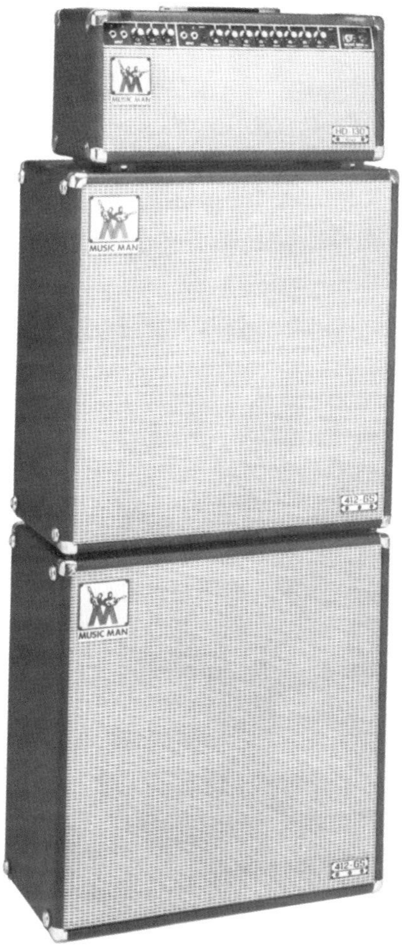

From Amplifier Catalog January 1,1979

Chapter 7

MUSIC MAN

And Then Some! Music Man Starts Over! It's a A Whole New Ball Game

In spite of Tom's heroic efforts, the company melt-down continued through the summer of 1983. The scattering of reps and employees took many directions. Reps that had come from retirement to join Music Man went back to retirement. Others changed business cards and moved on. Babe Simoni, as mentioned, opened his own business. Roger Balmer was recruited by the new Fender Company to promote a line of competitive sound systems. Mark Wentling, a valuable asset where ever he went, eventually joined associates Thom Brady and Paul Meisenzahl, taking over Uschi's former E and E Export Company. There I contacted him to discuss my D'Angelico project and later this book. Don Stouder, latched on to an RV enterprise. Dan Hoy and Connie collaborated in a silk-screen venture and Elisabeth Pedraza, now Meyer, grateful to Music Man for her introduction to Matteis Meyer and a happy marriage.

WORKING MUSICIAN

Working Musician logo

Two of the last to leave Music Man and suffered the most by its misfortune, were Jack Steele and Jody Carver; more about them later. By now, I had made a major move. On November 1st of 1982, it dawned on me, "you have all the experience you need to start your own independent rep company!" I wrote a list of names on a sheet of paper, looked them over, then crossed them out one by one until Working Musician remained. A visit to Customline Design and Bill McCartin's concept, produced the logo that has identified my professional activity ever since. Several product lines were available to me. The clincher came with a call from Dave Holcomb at GHS. "Frank! you're no longer at Music Man! What's going to happen to their string sales? I hear you're becoming an independent sales rep. What are the chances you can take on GHS?" This was all I needed to guarantee Working Musician's success! It was a unique situation in that Phil Hulsey, the respected original GHS west coast rep, had set up exclusive GHS Dealerships and would not go back on his promises. In the meantime 'brand name' competitors were selling strings to every possible store front; Records, Sheet music, Repair shops, Keyboard outlets and independent Music Lesson Studios.

My instructions were to contact legitimate small music retailers, of which Dave gave me a list of 150 in California and Nevada. Thus began a fascinating travelogue through every highway and bi-way in the two states, where there was, or might be, a prospective customer.Approaching NAMM Show time, January 21st, 1983, I had been on the road through most of the territory, visiting or opening nearly 100 accounts. Making GHS booth #343 my trade show base and passing by Music

Man on the way, was a strange feeling. I did visit Uschi at her E&E Exports booth, she was as charming and vibrant as ever. The traditional GHS show dinner at the Marriot Hotel Sunday evening, my first, was a special event. What a fabulous close-knit organization! Dave Holcomb's humorous sales report, punctuated by spontaneous digs from the career established reps and stabilized by beloved owners, Bob and Shirley McFee, was unforgetable! What a difference a year made; for Music Man and for me!

One of several incidents after Music Man, started from a phone call to my home based office. Any of us that knew Leo, were aware of his phone habits. He would often call when you least expected. He never identified himself. "Frank, I want you to come down here tomorrow!" You had better recognize his voice immediately, which came naturally early on. Leo was Leo! Nobody else sounded like him. Fortunately, my schedule was flexible. "What time do you want me there?" "9:00 AM!, click!" His phone conversations often ended abruptly. Next morning at ten to nine, I drove onto Fender Avenue, in Fullerton, off the 57 freeway. I parked close to building 'C' and went into the waiting room. The Secretary smiled and announced my arrival. Shortly, the door opened and George Fullerton beckoned me to follow him to the small, sparsely furnished conference room. Leo was waiting, seated at the table. We shook hands. "Frank, we want your opinion on this guitar; something separate from G&L, if you want to handle it." He leaned closer and lowered his voice. "Don't tell anyone about this project!"

George turned his chair, reached down and uncovered a guitar case behind him. Lifting it on to the table, he opened it slowly and took out the mystery guitar. It had a unique body style, somewhere between a Music Man Sabre and a conventional Strat. George tuned it, then handed it to me. There was no name on the headstock. I sighted the neck and neck joint, noted the lowered action and checked the harmonics. "Looks interesting!" I ventured. "Good!" Leo seemed pleased. George put the guitar back in its case, then on the floor under its cover out of sight. After conversation about other lines I was representing and key dealers in the territory, Leo repeated his opening request. "Don't tell any one about this project! No one else knows! We'll call you when we're ready to go!"

Driving back up the freeway, I reasoned, if this new line has to be unrelated to G&L, I can see why they need separate reps. The drama had just begun! Two days later, my phone rang. "Frank! It's Jack Steele! What's this about the new line your doing for Leo?" "What line?" I dodged. "Ca'mon Frank, I know you had a private session with Leo and George, the other day! You can tell me!" I couldn't lie to Jack. "Yes, I was down there. They showed me a no-name instrument. Nothing in the way of an agreement was put together. They said they'd get back to me when they were ready. They also stated, nobody knows any thing about this project and don't tell anyone! Jack was satisfied for the moment. I asked him how things were going? His reply was negative; his last words, "let me know what happens!"

There was more to come; next day another phone call. "Frank! Your East Coast Dodger die-hard, Jody. The word here on 48th Street, is that you are selling Leo's secret guitar. Is it true?" I recounted what I told Jack. It was obvious that the Leo/George secret guitar project was no longerprivileged information. I wondered if next month's trade magazines would disclose a special release, with my name involved!

I was concerned that Leo might think I leaked the story. Some years later, I had the opportunity at a NAMM Show to confront George Fullerton. I asked him if they thought I told my friends about the proposed secret guitar program. "No!" George laughed, "one of our own reps didn't understand the situation and how he would fit in. We decided to scrap the project!" Not much news came out of Music Man during 1983. My Working Musician rep operation was growing. I decided to have a booth at Summer NAMM in Chicago. I flew in two days early, my first trip to Chicago and walked up and down Michigan Avenue to get acquainted with the town. I liked it! My friend, Dean Brown (Frankfurt trip), came with me to help set up the booth. On Friday June 17th, we took a bus out to McCormick Place and located space #653. GHS had its own large booth. My small one was for my other lines: Centaur Systems, Strickland Stones, Stickspack, W/M Straps, Canare Cables and Torregano Gig Bags. The evening pre-show NAMM Mixer at the end of the Navy Pier came with a picture-perfect sunset. Looking back across the lake at the Chicago skyline was a memorable experience. The show dates. Saturday June 18th to Monday June 20th, were busy days, keeping us confined to the booth. If Music Man was there, I missed them. Who was left to write orders for what?

The last day of the year, 12/31/1983, was the last day for Music Man in Anaheim. Mark Wentling stayed until the end, His final paycheck was dated 12/30/1983. Babe Simoni and the factory crew packed up the tooling and equipment to be put in storage. No Music Man production amps have been built since. Jack Steele was unable to deal with the demise of Music Man. Whether he felt Tom could have made peace with Leo or secured other financial resources, I never found out. Jack had put everything into Music Man. He lost all of his insurance and retirement benefits. His bitterness turned him away from the music industry. I was sure I would see him at NAMM Shows or other musical events. I lost touch with him. Word had it, he was involved with a brother-in-law in Orange County, managing an apartment complex. He had been a good friend! I never heard from him again.

Jody Carver was a struggling survivor! Having been a very successful Fender Rep and steel guitar endorsement artist, like the others, the Music Man opportunity to be back with 'the old gang', was irresistible! He started with Tom's first Music Man opening in July of 1975 and stayed until the last days, selling Music Man close-outs. It was never easy for Jody, He had to turn down some of his old customers who wanted the Music Man line. Tom was emphatic against excessive discounting and trans-shipping, historically prevalent in 48th Street operations. Even though Jody promised to control their actions, Tom said, "No!". Alienation from 48th Street came back to haunt Jody, after Music Man, when he tried selling other lines. He was reduced to working at menial jobs outside the Music Industry for awhile, which proved a financial hardship. By June of 1984, Jody was back in Music Sales. He was too good to be out of the Music business. At the '84 Chicago Summer NAMM, I was meeting with a drum company from Taiwan, looking for representation. They shipped containers of drums to specified locations. The rep would take advance orders. The price was right! Everybody profited! Jody was interested. I sent him samples. We stayed in touch. As luck would have it, the wrong dealer got the shipment and Jody didn't get his cut! -

Jody Carver, steel guitar extraordinare playing his four neck Fender.

The chance to visit Jody came following the New Orleans NAMM Show, two years later. I flew into Kennedy Airport, rented a car and stopped by friends in Mahwah, New Jersey. The next day, Friday June 28th, 1985, 7:30 AM, I rendezvoused with Jody. I rode with him on his dealer calls. They were like 'story telling' sessions. Jody was always greeted with warm handshakes or hugs! There were orders already waiting for him, a look at new stuff and then the important part. "How's the family? Who won the ball game last night? Did Johnny get a hit? How was Aunt Susie's birthday party?".

Ernie Ball

Jody was casually dressed and relaxed. The day was more like a 'good will' tour than sales calls, but his brief case was full of orders! Jody invited me to spend the night at his beautiful home on Alyce Court in Somers, N.Y.. The house was surrounded by one of the biggest lawns, short of a golf course, I've ever seen; disappearing into it's own 'Sherwood forest'. "How do you cut all this grass?", I marveled! "Nothing to it!", Jody boasted, "I just crank up the 'super-jet-mower' and hang on!".

The Carver household, with Jody and his lovely wife, Marilyn, was warm and friendly, including a steel guitar performance in the family room. The 'ups and downs' of Jody's professional life culminated in one of his finest accomplishments; induction into 'The Steel Guitar Player's HALL OF FAME!", along side his 'role model', Noel Boggs!! Jody will have more to say about Tom Walker, but we must return to the end of 1983, moving into 1984, when Ernie Ball stepped in to bring new life to Music Man and his dear friend Tom Walker. As we all know, Ernie Ball revolutionized the guitar string business. Wayne Charvel tells the story: "When I was playing in bands in the early 60's, we wanted to emulate our recording heroes and 'bend' strings! Playing with a standard set of nickel wound electric light gauge, was like bending a barb wire fence. How did they do it? I found out! You had to buy two sets of strings; one the 12 gauge lights, the other a banjo set. You threw away the E6th from the light set. Now, the 5th string became the 6th. You pulled the .009 from the banjo set and made that your high E first string. That did it! You could bend strings with the Pro's"! Ernie Ball figured this out before the other string companies. He was our champion. We only had to buy one set, 'Slinky's or 'Super Slinky's'!

I only saw Ernie Ball once or twice. The first time had to do in keeping up with the demands of the 'string benders'! My Music Store in Sierra Madre sponsored several garage bands for participation in the Standel Wall of Sound, a Frank Garlock presentation. The bands had to have Ernie Ball strings! Ernie had a retail music store over in the Valley and began buying strings in bulk, probably from GHS at first, then coiling and packaging them in the back room. I would drive over and pick-up string orders. Ernie was also an established recording artist, a Fender Dealer with Tom Walker as his rep, plus in demand, as a respected guitar instructor.

A young Johnny Thompson accepts his award for his-contest winning performance of "The Steel Guitar Rag!"

My long time friend, Johnny Thompson, owner of J.T. Music in Monterey Park, was a pre-teenage student of Ernie's. Tom Walker heard Johnny play and followed his progress to winning the Fender Guitar Solo Contest, with his blazing performance of 'The Steel Guitar Rag'! Tom and Johnny became friends. Tom told me the story: I was amazed by John's talent as a player, but even more so, by his business acumen. He called me one day, still only a teenager, *"I've opened a music store!"*, When I went to visit his first small location, I thought, how can he afford a Fender Franchise? Johnny pulled a large roll of bills out of his pocket. *"I've been teaching guitar lessons in my bedroom for the last few years and saved the money!"* Tom finished his story, Johnny is a unique individual with an outstanding character. He never missed a payment, was always considerate and a loyal friend!

I met Sterling Ball for the first time in the late 60's or early 70's. By now Ernie was out of retail, had moved to Costa Mesa and national string and accessory distribution, focused on getting his own string winding machines and looking at property in San Luis Obispo for future expansion. This energetic, late teens, young man came into my store, hair tied back, looking like he just came from the beach. "I'm Sterling Ball! Your store has been selling a lot of our strings. I'm stopping by to check your operation and see how we can help promote more business!". Sterling was already previewing his future, when he would push the company to new promotional success and take Music Man guitars and basses to the quality levels that Tom envisioned. I didn't see Sterling again until I was employed at Music Man and he dropped by with Jimmy D'Addario to discuss our bass string packaging and update Tom on their band. Another five or six years passed before I chanced to sit beside Sterling on a return flight from Chicago NAMM. We chatted about industry changes since he visited my store as a teenager, in Sierra Madre.

By now he was a mature presence in the Ernie Ball Company. I asked him if we would ever see Music Man amps again? He thought about it briefly. "Timing!", he mused. "Timing is everything in the Music Industry as everywhere else. Now is definitely not it for amps; maybe a couple of years down the road!"

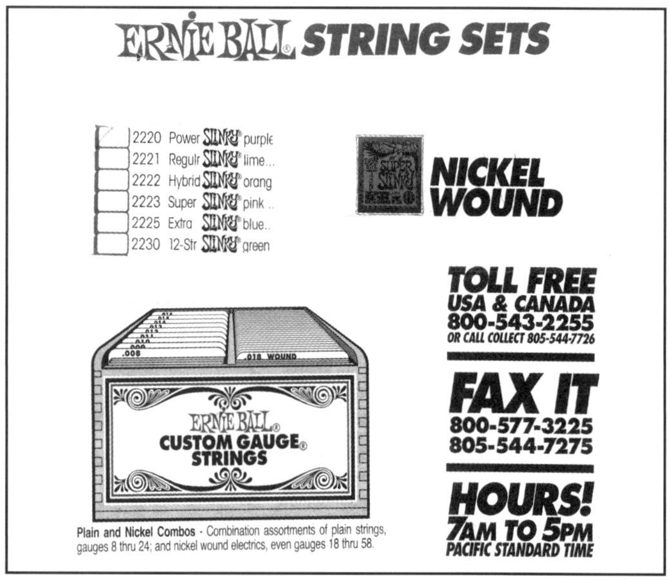

Highlights from an Ernie Ball mailer

In the Music Trades Magazine, November 2000 issue, a smiling Sterling Ball is pictured playing the latest Ernie Ball guitar. The article, 'Getting Ready For The Biggest Guitar Boom Yet', quotes; "Sterling Ball is convinced the guitar is more popular than ever!" His cross country rolling stage and record smashing 'Battle Of The Bands' promotions are actions to confirm his predictions. When Tom and his wife Pat moved up North to a peaceful, upper-class home, not far from Ernie's factory, those of us who knew Tom, were pleased that he could live a normal quiet life. Working on projects for Ernie, with his ever-present garage R&D lab, kept him occupied. Tom was never one to waste time sitting in a lounge chair. Mark Wentling did some Stingray Bass pre-amp refinements for Ernie, but eventually had to move on. Bill Schultz re-ignited the Fender Company, salvaging it from CBS, in 1985 and had an opening in their R&D department for Mark.

Looking back at his experience with Music Man, Mark recalls, "Back on July 23rd, 1979, I will always remember Music Man as 'Camelot!'. I first met Tom Walker a month or two earlier. I was working as a project engineer at MXR Innovations in my home town of Rochester, N.Y.. One of our graphic designers, Jim O'Rourke, confided in me that he was planning to have a job interview with Tom in Buffalo, N.Y..(about 90 miles away) and that Tom had asked Jim if he knew of any engineers interested in moving out to Music Man in California. I went along to Buffalo for the interview to see what would happen. We met at a motel. Tom was there with his Canadian rep out of Ontario, named Jim Kindness. I was immediately struck by Tom Walker's Texan smile and the ever-present twinkle in his eye. Tom was a real people person and even though he was quite a bit older than me, he was energetic, in that he exuded a real excitement about his future vision for Music Man, Inc.."

"I was an active bass player, but had not really noticed Music Man gear before. My background over the years had been building effects at MXR and making my own PA and lighting equipment through high school and college. I really knew very little about designing guitar amps. That did not seem to bother Tom. We hit it off very well right from the start. He wanted to make me his chief-engineer and offered a Southern California salary to boot. I couldn't wait to make the move! They flew me into Anaheim to look over the plant. I met Babe Simoni and toured the amp factory, then met Leo Fender and toured his guitar works. I met Roger Balmer, who Tom had recently brought in from Yamaha USA. Roger had worked at Yamaha with Bill Schultz (of Fender fame) during the era where they created the PM-1000/2000/3000 Series mixers and quite a bit more "big" PA -- gear plus they developed

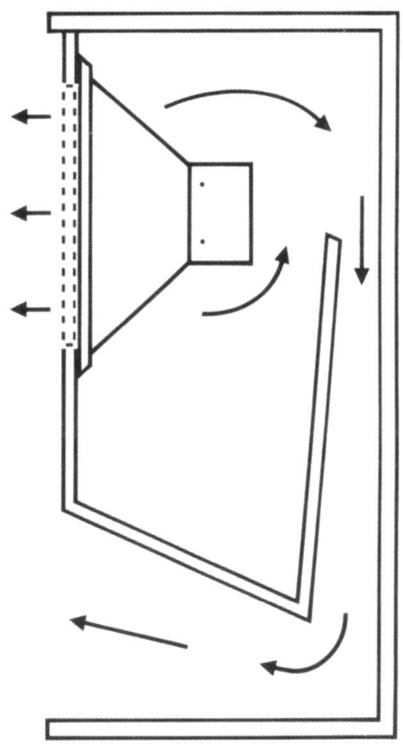

The Reflex Horn Speaker System is essentially a front loaded bass reflex enclosure whose port has been replaced with a folded horn. It is not be confused with the rear loaded folded horn (W Box), which is extremely efficient in the bass register but lacks the necessary treble response to provide adequate presence and definition.

(From the Amplifer Catalog January,1979)

Photos illustrate complete manufacturing facilities at Music Man amplifier plant. Much of the machinery and tooling was especially designed to improve the methods of fabricating various amplifier components. All sheet metal and cabinetry is produced internally to guarantee complete quality control.

instruments and the G(guitar) and B(bass) Series Yamaha combo amps. These amps had solid-state power amp modules and parametric EQ, which was unique at that time. This was a period where the US division of Yamaha played a big part in setting the direction for all Yamaha 'backline' combo gear and professional PA equipment. I was told a key part of the process was accomplished by retaining high profile consultants to guide the work; Stan Miller, Cal Perkins, John Windt, Mark Engebretson and Steve Wooley all participated in the PA program. John Carruthers and Paul Rivera both worked the guitar/amp program along with several others. Roger Balmer was smooth and very adept at networking with top-notch consultants. Unfortunately, using consultants eventually played a part in the break up of Music Man, Inc.."

Mark Wentling

Mark continues, "I didn't spend any time looking around Orange County, which surprised Tom. I knew I wanted to move right away! I learned that Tom Walker received his electronics training as a ham radio operator. When he came to California, he was part of a group who worked for Francis Hall at his business, Radio-Tel. They sold electronic components and performed repairs. Radio-Tel also distributed Fender gear and as Fender grew, Francis saw the growing market potential. He bought a company for himself, which would become Rickenbacher Musical Instruments; still owned and operated by his son, John Hall. Through this connection, Tom first met Leo Fender. He became Leo's second west coast salesman, following the untimely death of Charlie Hayes in a car accident on State College Boulevard."

"The incredibly vibrant California market established strong friendships through Tom's Fender Dealerships. Ernie Ball, a popular session player, store owner and guitar instructor, developed a unique relationship with Tom, as close to 'family' as possible, which one day would play an important role in Music Man's survival. Years later, when Music Man was up and running, virtually all the amplifier concepts and designs came from Tom, with some collaboration, on later models, with myself (Mark). The original Music Man amps used EL-34 tubes in the outputs driven by a single 12AX7, that provided gain and phase splitting. Without proper cooling the EL-34's would overheat and fail. Tom borrowed an idea from radio transmitter design and came up with a Class B drive circuit, which used transistors to drive cathodes of the output tubes, instead of the traditional grid drive. This allowed him to use lower cost, sturdier 6L6G output tubes in place of the EL-34's. He also did away with the 12AX7.

The new approach picked up more power output. The 65 watt model bumped to 75 watts and the 130 watt to 150 watts. Further-more, he was able to make a 100 watt design which ran off only two 6L6G output tubes. This was twice that of conventional two tube Class A/B design capability. There was a trade-off to be made. These amps were clean and loud. Albert Lee, an endorser, could take your head off with his Telecaster played through his 410HD-150EVM, perfect for Albert's style, but too clean for players who loved the sound of the original 12AX7 with EL34's, warm and loose, even more so as the master volume was turned down and the negative feedback actually decreased, (a unique feature of the original Music Man designs).

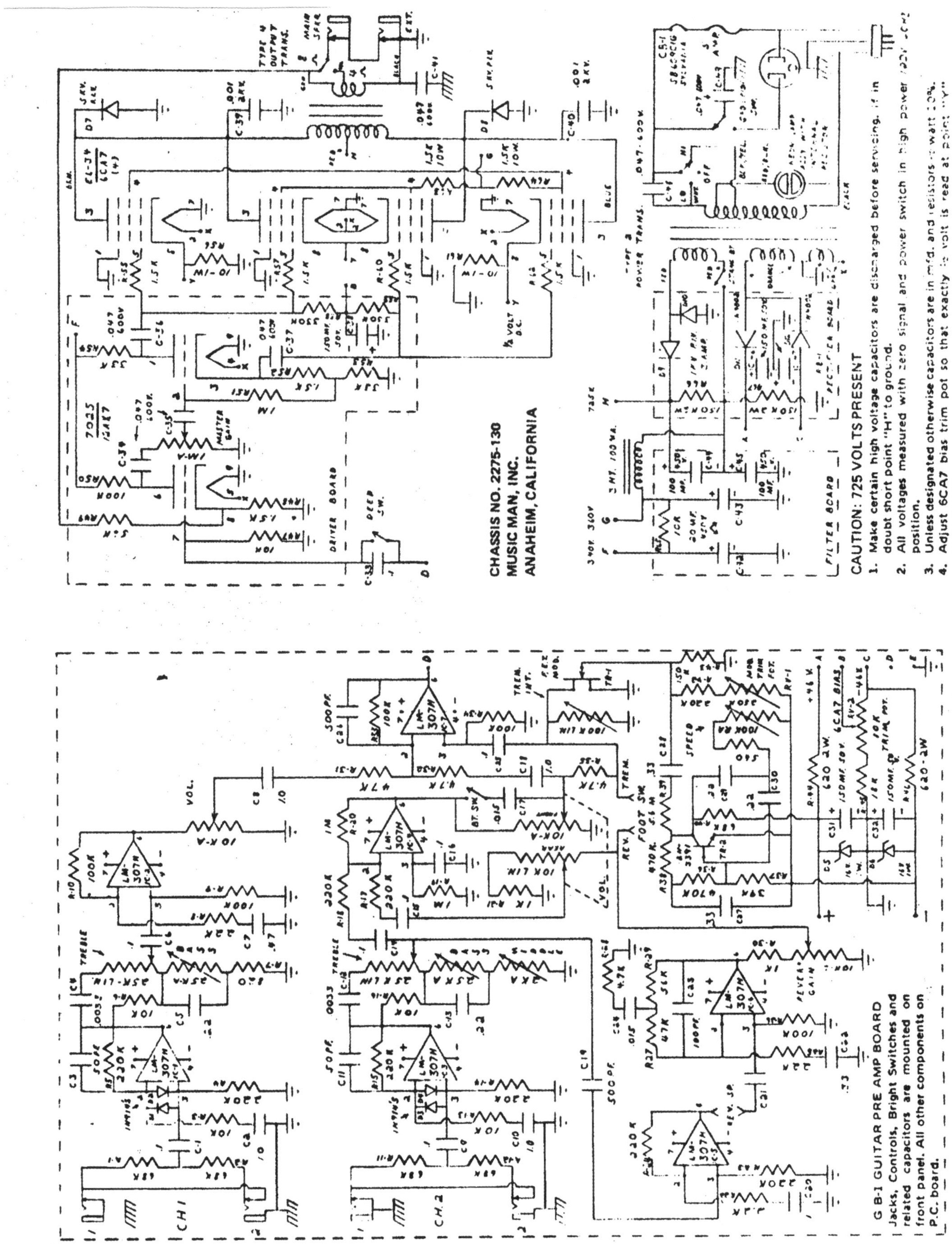

CHASSIS NO. 2275-130

Looking back, we probably could have kept the original designs and simply added fans on the tubes.!"

Mark's valuable in-sights, may result in a book of his own, when his busy schedule permits! Mark adds to his narrative: "To be honest, I learned so much from Tom, Babe and the others in the factory. I had never designed or built guitar amps from scratch before coming to Music Man. I also received mentoring from Paul Rivera, who Roger brought in to consult with us when I first arrived. Paul was very active in the LA area. He had many top-name clientele for his modification and repair business. He gave me some very good tips. I learned about speakers from Bob Gault, the founder of Eminence. Bob and Tom were very close friends and both were avid golfers. Tom sent me to Chicago to learn transformers from Ernie Smith and Bob Iverson at Schumacher Electric.

Tom and Pat Walker's San Luis Obispo home.

Another important thing I learned from Tom: his hand picked sales force, big overseas distributors, to whom he was so close; how to run business in a forthright, respectable manner! Tom was the consummate professional, yet always maintained his warm Texan affability. He often took time out in private to explain the ethics behind his decisions, providing a background and foundation how Music Man, Inc., did business. Tom always took the high road; with customers, employees, suppliers and partners. Tom was honest to a fault and always a gentleman. His word was his bond!" As mentioned previously, Mark Wentling and I, on occasion had reason to talk to each other. Possibly at the NAMM Show in Anaheim, January 2001, or shortly there after, we criticized the books and magazine articles circulating stories relative to the 'rise and fall' of Music Man. Tom Walker was either blamed for its failure or ignored for its accomplishments; such as the design and manufacture of Music Man amplifiers, the finest of the time, on their introduction to the music industry; some still in service and much searched for by knowledgeable players and collectors. I mentioned to Mark I had accumulated material for possibly writing, 'The Truth About The Music Man Story' and Mark replied, "I've considered it myself!". We decided the best approach would be to drive up to San Luis Obispo and visit Tom. It was a great idea!. Mark still kept in touch with Tom from time to time. I hadn't seen him in over ten years! We set April as a date our schedules would coincide.

Mark called Tom and set a date for lunch on Saturday April 21st. I left a day early to make sales calls in Santa Barbara on the way, spending the night in Buelton. Mark drove up on Saturday morning, bringing his family. Tom wanted to see Mark's children, the youngest for the first time. We all arrived at the Walker's lovely home by 12:00 noon. If you judge a man by his wife, Tom rates an A+! Pat Walker is a wonderful homemaker, her background in interior decorating, reflected in their home. We spent an hour catching up on events leading to the present. The subject of a book about Tom's contributions to the music business entered in the conversation. I presented Tom with a copy of 'The Custom Guitar Shop and Wayne Charvel', to let him know, his story was not my first attempted biography. He browsed through the book, chuckling at the picture of Wayne meeting Leo. He looked up at me momentarily, "I don't think I'm all that important! Ernie (Ball) should be the first to write his story. If I'm in it, that will be enough!" Mark and I talked about this later. We agreed this was

Lunch at the Apple Farm. Left to right; Tom Walker, Pat Walker, Mary Desidario, Mark's mother-in-law, Janet Wentling, Mark's wife, holding baby Angela; David, Stephen, Desi and Mark Wentling. The empty chair, is for the photographer, yours truly!)

not the time to go ahead with a Music Man publication.

Tom made a reservation for all of us at the popular 'Apple Farm Restaurant'. This was Mark and my treat! We had a great lunch, afterward going for a walk at the Mission and sitting by the deep running, tree shaded stream. It was a heart-warming, memorable day; the last time we would see Tom Walker!

Two years later, on August 20th, 2003, I received an e-mail from Jody Carver titled, "Good Bye to another Fender original!" He wrote, *"This past Friday AM, my friend Tom Walker and former original salesman, made his last call. He was called by God! He was Leo's first ever salesman on the West Coast and was responsible for the Fender success story as much as anyone on the Fender team. It was he who introduced Noel Boggs to Leo Fender and it was he who was the driving force and friend of all the Fender dealers he called on over the years. It was he who introduced Mary Kaye and Wayne Newton to Leo. It was he who created many Fender products along with Leo and yet few people are aware of this. He resigned from CBS Fender in 1969. It was he who convinced Leo to return to the business he loved so much! It was he who worked along with Leo and Forrest White, to form the Music Man Company.*

It was he who designed the Music Man amp and it was he who convinced me there was another world outside of CBS Fender. It was he who passed away this past Friday, quietly in his sleep! Just a few days before, I spoke to him for the last time. He was and still is my friend and former boss. God rest his soul! Rest in peace my friend! Jody Carver.

Jody spoke for all of us! - Tom and Pat Walker.

To this day, as I continue to call on dealers and attend trade shows, Tom's many friends offer stories and pictures relevant to Music Man. Lightning Joe's Guitar Heaven, a family run store, in Arroyo Grande, California, has my vote for one of the best Guitar Retailers on the planet; a must visit destination, if you're in the area. Lightning Joe Daoust's guitar expertise is second to none. Marelene manages the counter operation, a 'breath of fresh air', charming and capable;

Joey, a college bound honor student, wearing his Ernie Ball 'T' shirt and sitting on one of their Music Man collectibles and little Savanna, runs around with a million dollar smile. Lightning Joe's is known for its custom setup guitars and vintage instruments; always on the lookout for Music Man equipment. The recently opened stairway up to second floor guitar-heaven, features a classroom, souvenir shop, museum, mini-concert hall and coffee time; a perfect place for the Music Man (and lady) to visit.

Lee Lowe, of Lowe's Music in Newhall, California, protectively shows off his prized Music Man 112-RD.

Tracy Sands, electronics whizz, recalls his productive employment at the Music Man amp factory and later on, a short-lived venture with Forrest White, 'The White-Sands Electronic Instrument Company'.

The Fret House in West Covina, CA, one of the world's finest guitar organizations! Reuben Ramos, touring pro-bassist and instructor; along side Tom Seymour, Fret House owner; displaying their 20+ year old Music Man gauged string boxes, good as new!

John Nelson and son, Chris of 'Vintage Gear' in Hollywood, CA. with their collectible Music Man Stingray Bass, circa 1978-81. The bass was previously played in the band, 'Prowler' as identified on the case shown below. John Nelson began collecting his guitars as a teenager in and all around the Long Beach area of Southern California. After tours with Eddie Money and his own band, 'Half Nelson', he focused on a livelihood of vintage guitar brokering. I first met John at Dean Brown Music in Arcadia, California, during the late 70's, while I was at Music Man. John Nelson was the store's inside/outside contact with the 'headline' groups of the day, in particular, our local product, Van Halen, to whom he demo'd and sold two HD-130 Music Man heads to power his concert hall Marshall speaker cabinets!

There was no further thought about a Music Man book at this point. We were looking forward to what Ernie Ball might write. Material for our future project continued to show up. A Wayne Charvel request, prompted a call to Bob Luly in Colorado. I had heard mention of his name, but never knew who he was. Wayne told me, "Bob Luly is an electronics genius. When he was a young guy in the LA area, he could fix or design any piece of equipment you needed. Leo Fender hired him for awhile and Bob can tell you stories, I don't believe, anyone else knows!". I gave Bob a call recently. A young voice answered the phone, "Who's calling?", I identified myself as referred by Wayne Charvel, regarding a Music Man book and tribute to Tom Walker. When Bob picked up the phone, he thanked me for calling. "Tom Walker was a fine man and special friend; honest, straight forward and reliable. He was a capable electronics engineer, always probing for improvements in product design. I was hired by Leo Fender before Music Man, when Leo, Tom and Forrest had formed a research group called 'Tri-Sonics'. They were looking into the new, proposed concept, of a solid-state/tube approach to building a guitar amp. Leo said, " "It can't be done without an overriding 'hum'!"" I suggested respectfully, I believe it can!" Leo was not convinced, "You'll have to prove it to me! Make me one!" So Bob did, solving the grounding problem that caused the 'hum'. When Bob brought the proto-type in for evaluation, Leo looked at it dubiously, "Plug in this guitar and turn the power on!" Bob did! No 'hum'! Leo reached over and cranked up the volume. Still, no 'hum'! He turned to Bob, "How in the world did you do it?"

As we all know, when Music Man debuted it's new amplifier line, they were the best in the business. How much credit does Bob Luly deserve? He's really not concerned. He values the friendship with Tom Walker and the time spent with Leo. Bob's resume is a winner! He earned a teaching credential and went on to teach at U.C. San Bernardino. His ensuing career in satellite communications has been financially rewarding. He lives happily, with his family in Colorado.

Apparently, the reason we had not seen any writings or biography from Ernie Ball, could have been his disinterest, as Tom's was, in bringing up the past, or it could have been health. When Ernie passed away without much public awareness, we were shocked! Here was another Music Industry veteran and leader, crossing the barrier to a higher life. Now, the urgency for the Music Man Story was a reality. In combining the input from Jody Carver, Babe Simoni, Mark Wentling and myself we provide a perspective from four different segments of the company; Jody, reping on the East Coast, out in the field; Babe Simoni, submerged in manufacturing; Mark Wentling, wrestling with schematics in R&D and myself in the carpeted, air conditioned, people game, marketing department. The common bond that holds us together, is the music man, Tom Walker!

We trust, that when you read this book, you will join with us in a tribute to Tom!There will always be a MUSIC MAN!

"For the Music Man who hears the difference"

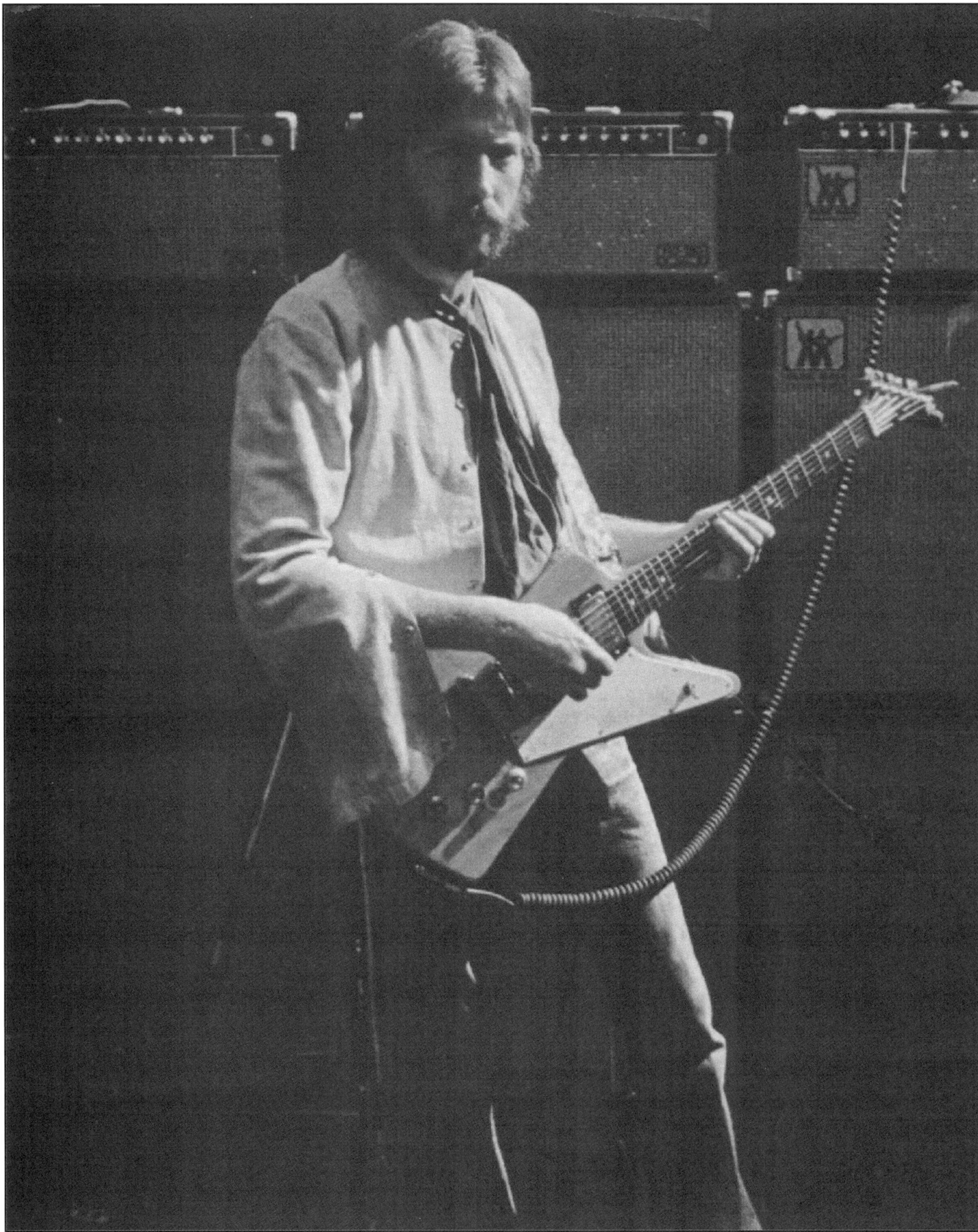

Eric Clapton with a wall of Music Man ampilfiers

The following 44 pages is from this January 1980 Catalog

Music Man — dedicated to helping musicians everywhere make more beautiful music.

Whenever it is time to develop a new catalog of Music Man products, I am reminded to make certain that we have everything in perspective. It is important that we at Music Man remember how we got here, and even more important that we not forget why we started out in the first place. Providing the best equipment for today's top instrumentalists seemed like a worthwhile objective back in 1972, and it seems equally so now.

All this reminds me of a warm Saturday afternoon back in the summer of 1974, when I was invited to bring some amplifiers over to the Long Beach Sports Arena. We had scarcely been in production a month, but already someone in the Eric Clapton organization had heard rumors of what we were up to. When we arrived and set up a couple of our 130 watt stacks, his roadie proceeded to arrange control settings while working with Eric's guitar and a couple of gain boxes. He explained that they required so much gain and sustain that amplifiers had been unable to provide it without help from outboard boxes.

An hour or two later, Eric appeared on the stage for a soundcheck, asked the roadie about the amplifiers, and received an affirmative nod. When the check was completed, he seemed pleased with what he heard, and asked to use our amps on the rest of his tour. Since the internal preamps of all Music Man amps are gain programmable (something new in those days), we were able to get rid of those external boxes much to the delight of his roadie.

To make a long story short, five Music Man heads and four stacks left town with them after the Sunday night performance. Those same five heads and four stacks have been on every tour for the past 6 years. Indeed, we had done what we started out to do: bring top equipment to a top artist so he could better express his talent to the audience.

This experience points out, once again, that progress does not begin until we begin to listen. Listen to the musician and listen to his needs. It takes a lot of listening to be Number One...and we are on our way.

Tom Walker
Tom Walker,
President

TABLE OF CONTENTS

AROUND THE WORLD WITH MUSIC MAN

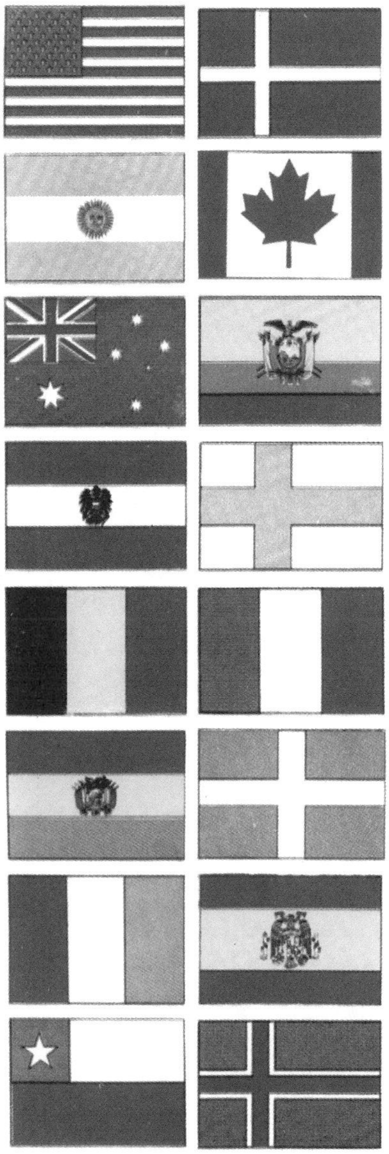

As more Music Man amplifiers appeared on concert stages around the world, we began to gain attention. Soon we reached the market with the Sting Ray Bass. It was new, it was different, and it brought a new dimension in sound to the bass player: more attention.

By early 1976 we began to appoint distributors. Switzerland, West Germany, England, Sweden, Denmark. Then France, Italy, Japan, Australia, New Zealand, Austria, Argentina, and so on. Forty-four countries in all. Now as many of our products are purchased overseas as are purchased here at home.

We take this opportunity to express our gratitude for the international acceptance of our instruments and amplifiers. That's what it's all about, helping musicians everywhere to make more beautiful music.

MUSIC MAN ELECTRIC GUITARS AND BASSES

SABRE I GUITAR
Fretted Maple Neck, Natural Finish

SABRE II GUITAR
Rosewood Fretboard, Black Finish

SABRE BASS
Fretted Maple Narrow Neck, White Finish

STING RAY BASS
Fretted Rosewood Neck, Sunburst Finish

MUSIC MAN INSTRUMENTS

We are proud to present this catalog of Music Man instruments. We believe they represent the essence of the most advanced techniques of the art, making use of the latest materials and the most modern manufacturing methods.

We have always been innovators, introducing products that are a little ahead of their time. For example, our designers and engineers were involved in developing some of the earliest solid body instruments. Now, as then, we find revolutionary ideas take some getting used to. Players initially had difficulty with the first solid body guitars because they no longer had a big box to use as an arm rest. When the first solid body basses came three years later, they were not generally accepted by bass players, so it was the guitarists who brought the instrument to prominence.

This same pattern of acceptance applies to the Music Man family of guitars and basses. Consider, for instance, our internal preamplifier. It brought to the performer a variety of sounds that never before were available. This time the bass players, not the guitarists, were among the first to recognize the advantages of the preamp. No longer were they saddled with a muddy rhythm sound that so easily tangles with the bass drum. Our preamp brought new clarity and definition to the electric bass, giving the instrument a distinct identity.

And take the guitarist, ever searching for new sounds as evidenced by the tremendous growth of the replacement pickup industry. They buy new pickups to get more power, more drive and sustain, or more treble or bass — or whatever. Given reasonably good basic pickups, all these things can be done electronically, and often better.

The recording and concert business has fostered revolutionary techniques in EQ for microphones and instruments. A little of that technology at your fingertips, within the instrument, can be a step in the right direction.

Ultimately, you don't get something for nothing. Many manufacturers have attempted to reduce the price of their instruments by adopting automated mass production methods. This is healthy for the industry because at least some of these instruments bring acceptable performance to the player who cannot yet afford a truly professional model. One should not be taken in, however, by such theories as "a neck is a neck." A neck cannot be made as well in 90 seconds on an automatic machine as can be done manually by a true craftsman. Many such hidden costs are necessary when producing a top professional instrument. It literally is true that when you're dealing with a quality oriented firm, you *do* get what you pay for.

EVERY PART OF A MUSIC MAN INSTRUMENT IS SPECIAL

TUNING MACHINES

The tuning keys are precision built by Schaller to our specifications, including heavy nickel plating. These high-ratio machines use Music Man's patented tapered string post that ensures the string always winds down tight to the headstock. The post is slotted and drilled to allow for fast string insertion with a positive grip. Backlash is minimized by a self-tensioning mechanism and a special case hardened steel ferrule located at the base of the string post; machined to be perfectly round, the ferrule has an internal bearing surface that reduces friction.

NECKS

The neck and head are formed from a single piece of hard rock maple, with grain running straight from end to end. One-piece construction not only makes a far stronger neck, it is less apt to warp or twist than a laminated neck. Moreover, this approach provides a consistent wood cell structure throughout the neck so expansion and contraction remain symmetrical in changing environments, vibrational characteristics are more uniform, and truss rod adjustments are smoother. (An ABS bushing protects the headstock during truss rod adjustments.) The truss rod is a patented Music Man flat design yielding greater strength with a thinner neck.

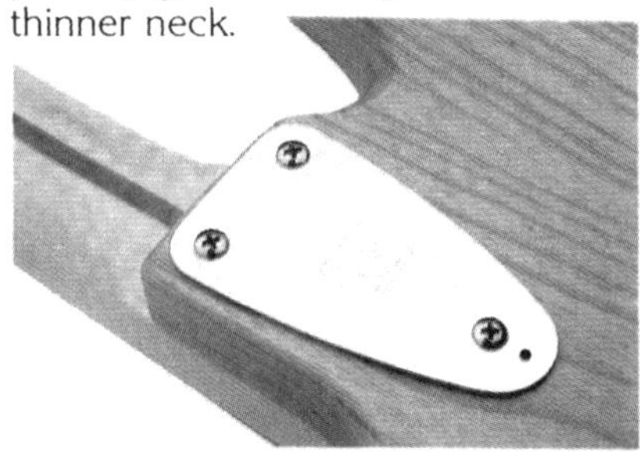

The angle between the neck and body is adjustable by means of a convenient screw. Thus, a player can readily set the neck tilt for best results with any desired string type or action height preference, with no special shims.

NUTS

We use rock-hard melamine nuts, a polymer material that can be precision notched, minimizes friction for smooth tuning, and provides long wear.

FRETBOARDS

On instruments with rosewood or ebony fretboards, the fretboard is neither a thin veneer nor a flat block glued to the maple and then shaped. Instead, we built a special machine that carves a block of rosewood or ebony into a pre-curved constant-thickness fretboard. The fretboard is then applied to the curved maple neck, a technique that minimizes

warp or twist problems that are otherwise encountered when using dissimilar woods. Again, our approach is more costly, and far more effective than the alternatives.

FRETS

Music Man frets are made of an extra hard nickel-silver alloy for longest wear, inserted using a proprietary technique that locks them in place and prevents lifting. A minimum of material is removed during fret filing so as to maintain a rounded profile, hence reduced contact against the strings for more precise intonation. The fret edges are dressed to allow the maximum useable fret width on the fretboard for the widest string bending range. At the same time, the edge contour is more than adequate for comfortable, snag-free action as your hand moves along the fretboard.

BODY

Our guitar and bass bodies are light weight, well balanced to the neck, and contoured for player comfort. We use only select woods, ash or poplar, thoroughly seasoned to optimize the moisture content for reduced sensitivity to adverse environmental changes. We cut the wood into large strips and then glue them back together so that stresses are balanced. This prevents warpage or cracking and is far more durable than a single-piece body.

FINISH

All instruments are finished exclusively with lacquer. Alternatives, such as polyurethane and polyester, tend to stick to the skin, are more prone to cracking under adverse weather conditions, tend to shatter when struck, and are virtually unrepairable. Lacquer allows your hand to glide smoothly up and down the neck, can be repaired, and tends to age better. Due to the increased preparation and longer drying time, lacquer costs more than other finishes, but we feel its advantages justify the cost.

PICKUPS

Music Man anti-hum pickups are designed for the widest possible frequency response, maximum sustain and a "fat" full sound. They contain specially designed magnets that are powerful, yet not so strong they distort the natural orbit of the string or cause beating. We refuse to use automatic machines that wind a number of pickups simultaneously because the winding tension must be reduced so that none of the multiple windings is broken — an unacceptable compromise. Instead, we do it the old fashioned way, 1 on

1; one operator manually winds one pickup at one time. A sense of touch develops and assures the very tightest possible winding. The result is less susceptibility to feedback due to "microphonic" pickups, and improved hum rejection due to better matching between coil pairs. We also lacquer each coil so it won't shift, even after years of touring and hard use.

PREAMPS

Music Man instruments all have a built-in active preamplifier. It consists of a plug-in integrated circuit (for reliability and serviceability) plus discrete components (for maximum gain and lowest signal-to-noise ratio), all powered by a single 9V battery. The preamp converts the pickups' high impedance to a low impedance that is able to feed longer cords without losses of signal strength or high frequencies. The preamp also provides greater compatibility with effects boxes than is presently available on most conventional guitars or basses. Because our instruments will put out more than double the level of instruments without a preamp, you can get maximum sound levels out of your amplifier with an excellent signal-to-noise ratio, or, you can intentionally create distortion and sustain by overdriving the amplifier.

While the premium output jack switches the preamp OFF when no plug is inserted, actually the preamp draws so little power that, even in continuous use, the battery will last for its rated shelf life of about 1 to 3 years. The preamp is designed so the sound gradually weakens as the battery nears the end of its useful life, giving you plenty of time to install a new battery without danger of sudden failure.

ABOUT SUSTAIN

Sustain describes how long the string and the instrument continue to vibrate when you play a note. It is one of the most talked-about and least understood factors in the design of a guitar or bass — everyone wants more sustain, yet with a controlled response that avoids acoustic feedback. In this catalog, and elsewhere, you will see discussions about how one feature or another increases sustain. Individually, these features do indeed contribute to the sustain, but bear in mind that sustain does not result from any one or two features of an instrument. Many factors that contribute to sustain: the rigidity of the neck, the types of neck and body materials and how they are assembled, the mass of the bridge assembly, the construction of the truss rod, the hardness and shape of the nut and frets, the pickups, electronics, and so forth. Even the finish can affect sustain to some extent.

Truly satisfactory sustain depends upon everything, all the features, working together in unison. At Music Man we understand every nuance of sustain, and, accordingly, we make subtle adjustments in our designs to maximize the performance of each guitar and bass.

QUALITY CONTROL

All Music Man electric guitars and basses pass through numerous strict quality control check points during the manufacturing process and again during final assembly. Once the instrument has passed all preliminary tests, it goes on to a team of skilled guitar technicians for a final quality control check. This extra step is taken to ensure that each instrument meets all of the set-up and performance specifications that we so carefully established.

Only those instruments that successfully complete all the tests are released to authorized Music Man dealers.

SABRE
GUITAR

SABRE GUITAR

Each of the Sabre guitars offer the professional player tremendous flexibility to suit individual playing styles, action preferences, and string selections. While the Sabre I and II differ in their neck curvature and fret shape, they are otherwise identical. No detail is too small to receive our close attention, and they all add up to create an impressive instrument. Each guitar is crafted by hand and by special precision machinery designed and built with Music Man expertise. And each is registered, with the serial number stamped on the bridge. The instrument body is contoured to fit most players for greatest comfort. If the player takes a little time to learn how all the various controls work, he will obtain a variety of sounds not available on other instruments. With Music Man, you not only get your money's worth, you get a musical instrument of enduring quality.

SABRE GUITAR

THE NECK

Every part of a guitar is important, but certainly the neck has the greatest impact on the feel and action of a fine instrument. From the tip of the headstock to the last fret, Music Man necks are built to satisfy the playing requirements of today's top musicians.

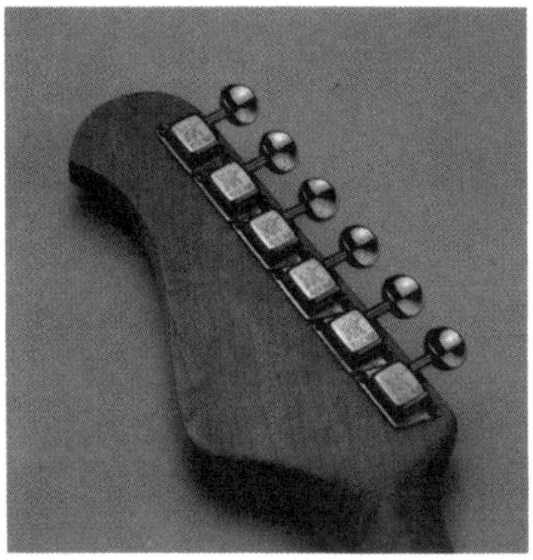

HEADSTOCK, TUNING MACHINES AND NUTS

The tuning machines are smooth and without backlash. Our patented tapered string posts guide the strings toward the headstock. A string retainer also holds down the top 3 strings, applying proper tension at the nut and shortening the effective string length between the nut and tuning post, which eliminates any tendency for unwanted sympathetic vibrations. The retainer is designed so that the strings cannot slip off accidentally.

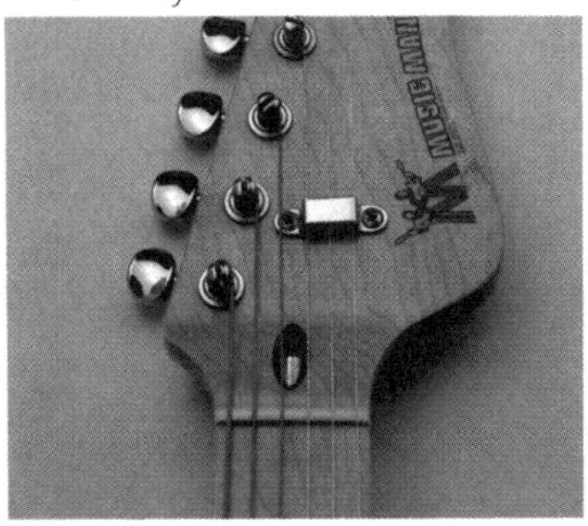

The neck and headstock are shaped so that the strings pull straight across the nut, not at an angle. The nut itself is precision notched to match the angle of the strings. This combination of design factors reduces the tendency of the instrument to go out of tune when you're bending strings, using a capo, etc. By allowing extra wood thickness, we add plenty of strength to the critical junction of headstock and neck.

FRETBOARD AND FRETS

We offer a choice of rosewood or maple fretboard material on both the Sabre I and Sabre II. The rosewood is unfinished, carved and applied with Music Man's constant thickness process. Maple fretboards are integral with the neck and are lacquer finished to match the rest of the guitar.

Both models have a 25-1/2" scale length and 22 frets. The two models differ only in neck and fretboard style. The Sabre I's fretboard has a 12" radius of curvature and jumbo frets for the player who likes to bend strings. The Sabre II's fretboard has a 7-1/2" radius with standard frets. (See illustration for fret profile.)

NECK CONSTRUCTION

The neck and head are formed of a single piece of select, hard rock maple, as described earlier. The neck measures 1.640" wide at the nut, 2.185" wide where it joins the body, and is 0.800" thick along its full length, offering a consistent, comfortable feel in any position.

The neck is cut square at the end that joins the body, and is seated tightly. This provides the optimum transfer of vibration between neck and body, increasing sustain. The specific method by which neck is bolted to the body minimizes side play and unwanted movement, preserving proper intonation.

THE BODY

The light weight body has a double cutaway that allows full access to all frets. Improved, deep-recess strap buttons provide positive grip on the strap and avoid enlarged strap holes for increased security.

BRIDGE

The bridge is a heavy diecasting. The unique Music Man string offset design allows the strings to pull through the lower end of the bridge casting where they are offset to force the saddles against the bridge, resulting in a rigid, vibration-free assembly that yields maximum sustain. The diecasting has a recessed well that houses the 6 individual bridge saddles and eliminates side-slipping. A second cast well on the bottom of the bridge is imbedded in the body and is designed to transmit the string tension to the end grain of the wood, anchoring the bridge to the body and further increasing sustain. The bridge saddles are made of stainless steel to resist corrosion, rust, etc. There are 2 stainless steel screws per saddle for individual height, and a third screw for individual string length. All screws are recessed within the saddle to avoid interference with picking or muting styles, and the entire

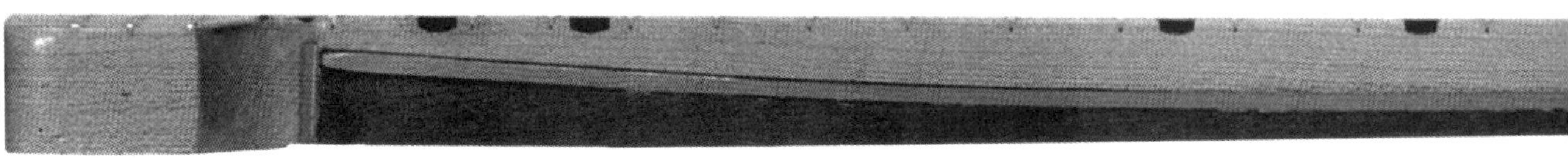

bridge assembly is designed to eliminate jagged or rough edges.

PICKUPS

Two hum cancelling, high output, shielded pickups are precisely mounted for lead and rhythm sounds. The pickups are tri-mounted to give a full range of vertical and tilt adjustments. Both pickups are individually sized to compensate for their position along the diverging strings and thus locate the magnetic pole pieces directly beneath their respective strings.

PREAMP

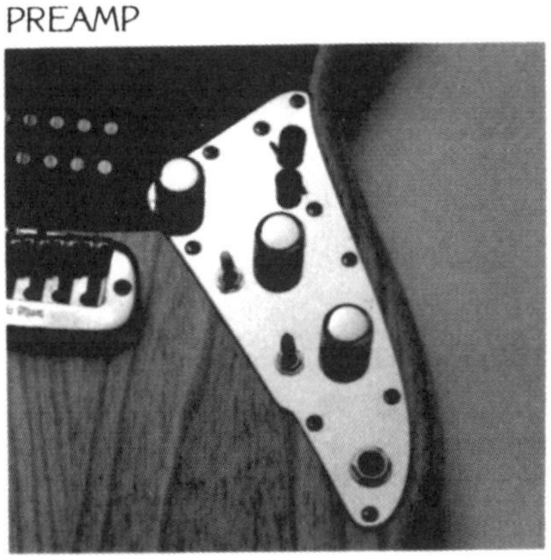

The Sabre's integral, battery-powered preamplifier makes separate tone controls possible, (one for treble and one for bass) while also eliminating interaction between tone and volume controls.

OUTPUT JACK

The preamp output is brought to a premium grade phone jack that securely holds the plug.

SELECTOR SWITCH

The pickup selector allows you to choose between the lead and rhythm pickup, or to use them in combination. This fast-action lever switch is positioned for ease of operation while you are picking.

PHASE SWITCH

The phase switch puts the lead and rhythm pickups out of phase with one another so that a positive pulse from one is cancelled by a negative pulse from the other. This results in a thin, bright sound. While many guitars require that the pickup selector switch be set in mid position for the phase switch to function, the Sabre's phase switch works with the pickup selector in any position; you only need to use one switch to get the phased sound.

BRIGHT SWITCH

The bright switch provides an instantaneous treble boost, and is useful for putting an edge on the pick attack.

FINISH

A handsome, and durable lacquer finish is applied to the neck and body. You have a choice of finishes, all glossy unless otherwise noted: natural, *satin* finish natural, sunburst (a 3-color burst), walnut, white and black.

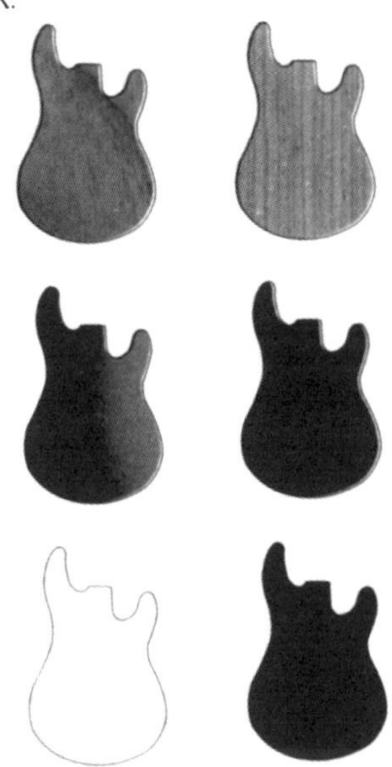

SABRE GUITAR SPECIFICATIONS

NUMBER OF FRETS:	22.
SCALE LENGTH:	25-1/2".
DIMENSIONS:	
OVERALL LENGTH	39-7/8" (1012.8 mm).
WIDTH AT WIDEST POINT	13" (330.2 mm).
OVERALL THICKNESS	neck, 0.800" (20.3 mm), body 1-5/8" (15.9 mm).
PICKUPS:	2 anti-hum type.
OUTPUT:	+7 dBv (2.3 volts) maximum into 10 kohms or higher load. +2.5 dBv (1.36 volts RMS) into 600 ohms.
BATTERY:	9 V alkaline, MN-1604 Mallory or equivalent.
FRET MATERIAL:	Nickel-silver alloy (18% nickel is very hard for long wear).
FRETBOARD INLAY:	Dot style on face and side.
WOODS:	
NECK	Hard Rock Maple.
FRETBOARD	Maple or Rosewood (per customer request).
BODY	Ash or Poplar (depending on finish).
NECK CHARACTERISTICS:	
SABRE I	Fretboard radius 12" (304.8 mm), jumbo frets.
SABRE II	Fretboard radius 7-1/2" (190.5 mm), regular frets.
FINISH:	High gloss lacquer (except as noted).
COLORS:	Natural, *satin* finish natural, sunburst, walnut, white, black.
HARDWARE:	All hardware heavy-duty chrome plated. Heavy-duty diecast bridge with stainless steel bridge saddles, individual string length adjustment and recessed saddle height adjustment screws. Tuning machines have patented tapered post: 14:1 ratio, self-tensioning.

Replacement parts and service are available from your Music Man dealer. These specifications are subject to change without notice or obligation.

StingRayBass

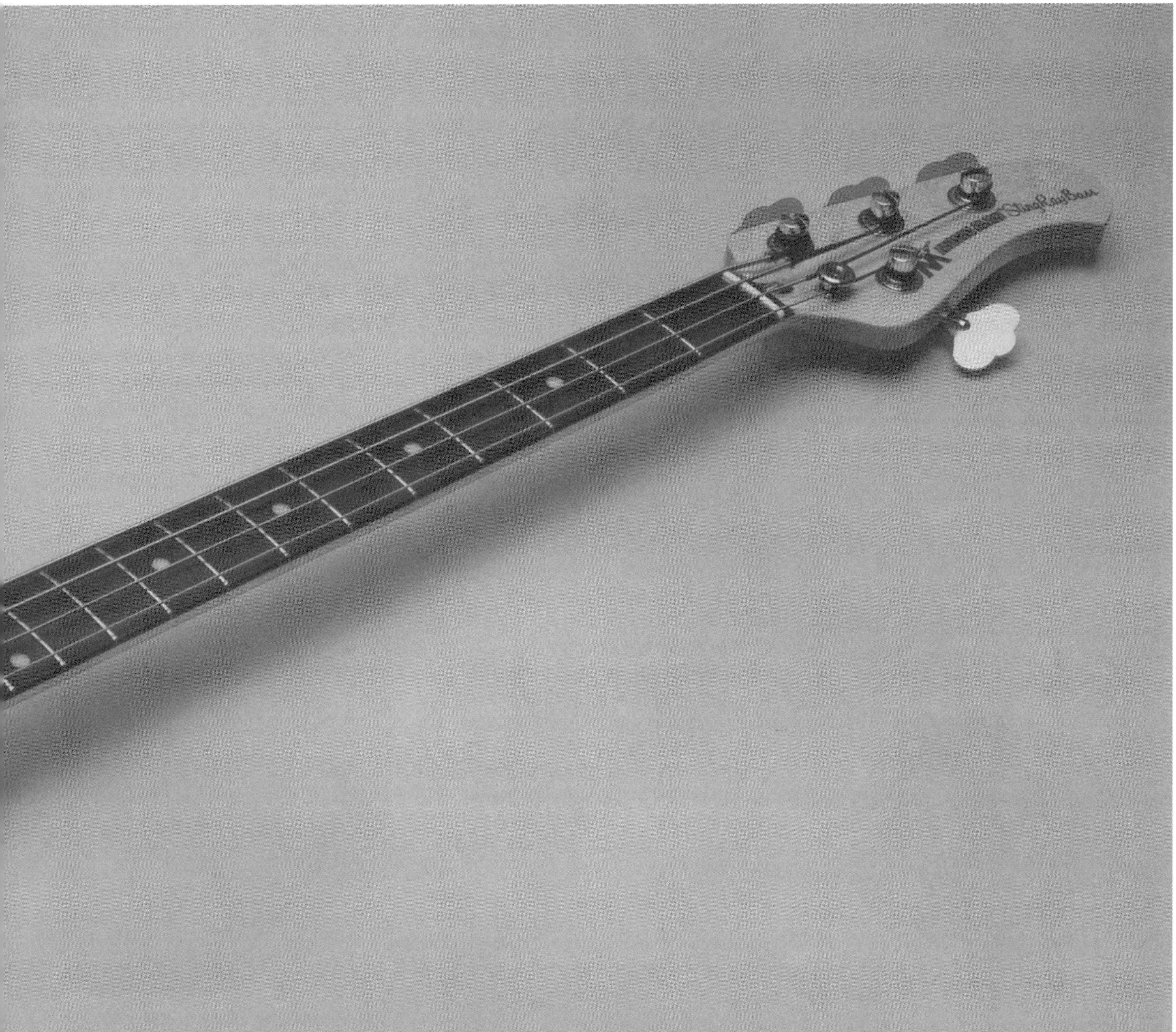

THE STING RAY BASS

"The Sting Ray is so versatile you can get almost any sound you want: from "clicky-pop" to a full, round bass — from warm and mellow to bright, biting, and punchy, but always startlingly clear. The Sting Ray has an extremely strong, clear midrange sound that always cuts through, so the bass part won't be lost in the shuffle. Even with the treble fully rolled off and bass fully on, the sound retains its excellent definition; it is never cloudy or thick. For studio work, the Sting Ray's distinctive tonality and built-in preamp mean you can plug directly into the recording board and, with very little EQ, if any, get the right sound onto the tape."

"The Sting Ray produces far more tonal variety than other basses when you pick the strings at different locations, yet the instrument is beautifully consistent in performance. Hot spots or dead spots are held to a minimum through careful neck design. Regardless of where you play on the neck or what type of strings you use, the harmonics "pop out" and the sound refuses to get muddy. The Sting Ray is somehow easier to play in-tune than most basses."

"The bass has superb physical balance, and is very comfortable to play. While it offers a full range of adjustments, it is very easy to set up. Using only an allen wrench, not shims, the neck tilt can be fully adjusted; make the strings nearly the same height at first and last fret, or set them for the angle that suits your personal playing style."

The Sting Ray bass has established itself as one of the most popular basses in the world today in a relatively short time. Since this bass was the first of our new generation of instruments, we are especially proud that many of the top international artists have selected this instrument for their playing enjoyment. The Sting Ray Bass — the new standard of sound.

STING RAY BASS

The Sting Ray Bass offers the professional player tremendous flexibility to suit individual playing styles, action preferences, and string selections. Whether you choose a fretted or the fretless model, the Sting Ray Bass is meticulously crafted by hand and by special precision machinery designed and built with Music Man expertise. And each is registered, with the serial number stamped on the bridge. With Music Man, you not only get your money's worth, you get a musical instrument of enduring quality.

THE NECK

The neck has the greatest impact on the feel and action of a fine instrument. The Sting Ray neck is fast, smooth and shaped for optimum playing comfort.

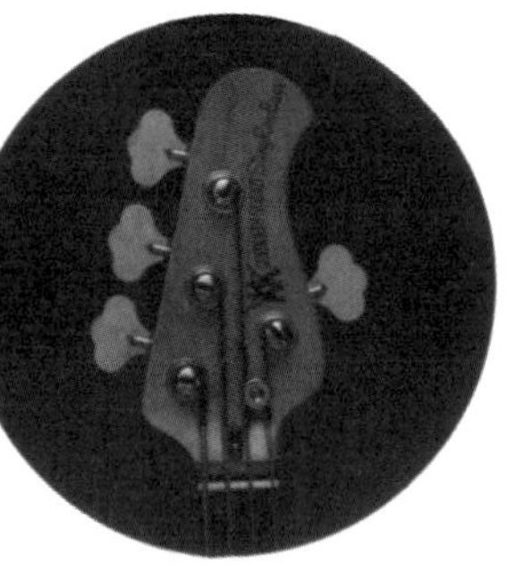

HEADSTOCK, TUNING MACHINES AND NUT

Like our other instruments, the neck and headstock are shaped so that the strings pull straight across the melamine nut, not at an angle. Additional benefits in common with our other instruments include the string retainer, which aids in applying proper tension at the nut, and Music Man's unique 3 and 1 headstock arrangement where the first string tuning machine is set on the opposite side of the headstock for better balance and shorter string end length.

FRETBOARD AND FRETS

We offer a choice of rosewood or maple fretboards on the Sting Ray Bass. The rosewood is unfinished, carved and applied with Music Man's unique constant thickness process. Maple fretboards are integral with the neck and are lacquer finished like the rest of the bass. (An ebony fretboard is standard on fretless models.) The Sting Ray Bass has a 34" scale with 21 jumbo frets. The fretboard's radius of curvature is 7-1/2".

NECK CONSTRUCTION

As with all Music Man instruments, the neck and head are formed of a single piece of select, hard rock maple for strength, resistance to warp or twist, and sustain. The truss rod is a patented Music Man flat design, one that yields greater strength with a thinner neck.

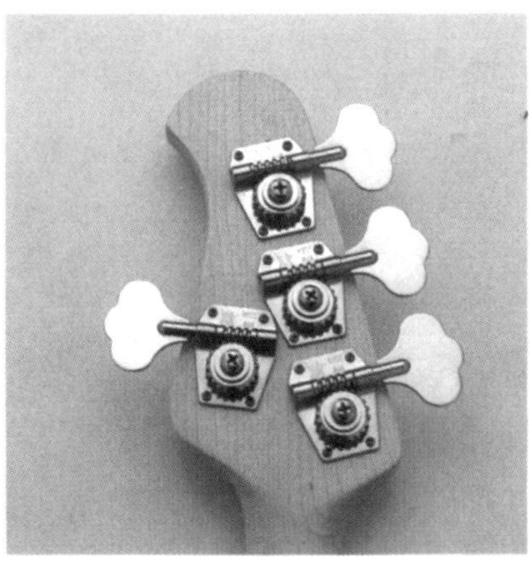

The neck is deeply seated where it joins the body, providing the optimum transfer of vibration between neck and body and increasing sustain. As with all Music Man guitars and basses, the neck tilt is screw adjustable.

THE BODY

The light weight, laminated ash or poplar body has a double cutaway that allows full access to all frets. Improved, deep-recess strap buttons provide positive grip on the strap and avoid enlarged strap holes for increased security.

BRIDGE

Strings pull through the rear of bridge and are routed to force the saddles against the bridge in a way

that maximizes sustain and eliminates unwanted vibration. The heavy tooled-steel bridge has two screws that fasten to brass inserts in the body, improving tone and increasing sustain. The bridge saddles are made of stainless steel to resist corrosion, rust, etc. In addition, there are 2 stainless steel screws per saddle for individual height, and a third for individual string length. All screws are recessed within the saddle to avoid interference with picking or muting styles, and the entire bridge assembly is designed to eliminate jagged or rough edges.

Another special feature of the Sting Ray Bass is that it has an individual mute for each string. These mutes are located just forward of the bridge saddles. Each is equipped with a thumb screw which adjusts the tension of the mute pad against the string. This allows you to change the degree of string damping to obtain different tonal characteristics.

PICKUP

A single, hum cancelling, high output, shielded pickup is tri-mounted to give a full range of vertical and tilt adjustments. This wide-response pickup provides maximum sustain and a "fat" or full sound.

PREAMP

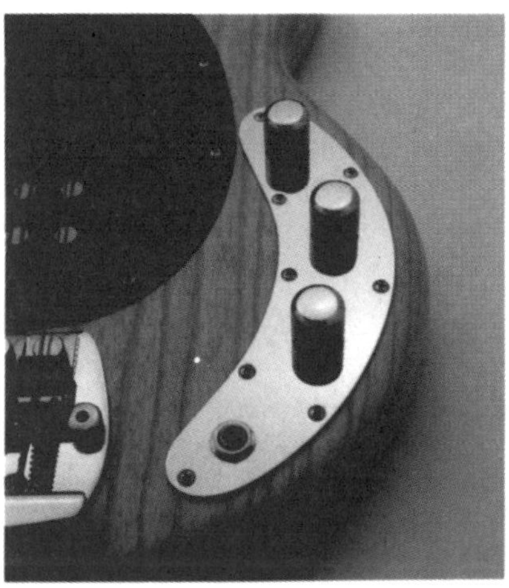

The integral, battery-powered preamplifier makes possible separate Bass and Treble boost/cut tone controls and a bright switch, while also eliminating interaction between tone and volume controls. The preamp's low impedance, high level output enables you to use longer cords without a signal degradation, and it provides greater compatibility with effects boxes and mixing consoles.

FINISH

A handsome, and durable lacquer finish is applied to the neck and body. You have a choice of finishes, all glossy unless otherwise noted: natural, *satin* finish natural, sunburst (a 3-color burst), walnut, white and black.

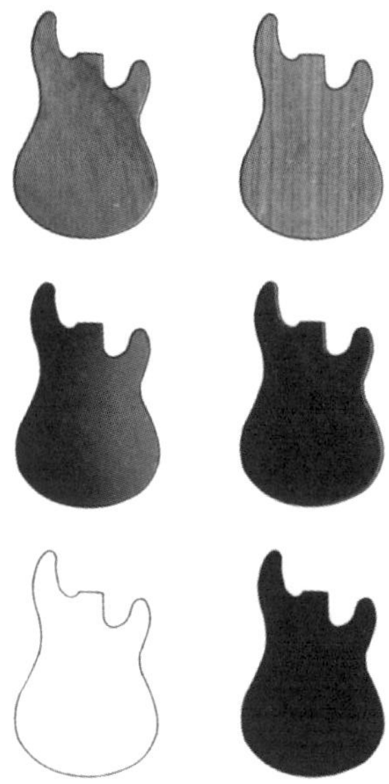

STING RAY BASS SPECIFICATIONS

NUMBER OF FRETS:	21.
SCALE LENGTH:	34" (864 mm).
DIMENSIONS:	
OVERALL LENGTH	45" (1143 mm).
WIDTH AT WIDEST POINT	13" (330 mm).
OVERALL THICKNESS	neck .800" (20.3 mm), body 1-5/8" (41.3 mm).
PICKUPS:	Single anti-hum type.
OUTPUT:	+7 dBv (2.3 volts) maximum into 10 kohms or higher load. +2.5 dBv (1.36 volts RMS) into 600 ohms.
BATTERY:	9 V alkaline, MN-1604 Mallory or equivalent.
FRET MATERIAL:	Nickel silver alloy (18% Nickel is very hard for long wear).
FRETBOARD INLAY:	Dot style on face and side.
WOODS:	
NECK	Hard Rock Maple.
FRETBOARD	Maple or Rosewood (per customer request). Ebony is standard on fretless models.
BODY	Ash or Poplar (depending on finish).
NECK CHARACTERISTICS:	7-1/2" (190 mm) fretboard radius. Jumbo frets.
FINISH:	High gloss lacquer (except as noted).
COLORS:	Natural, *satin* finish natural, sunburst, walnut, white, black.
HARDWARE:	All hardware heavy-duty chrome plated. Heavy-duty tooled bridge with stainless steel bridge saddles, individual string length adjustment screws. Tuning machines have patented tapered string post; 20:1 ratio and self-tensioning.

Replacement parts and service are available from your Music Man dealer. These specifications are subject to change without notice or obligation.

SABRE
BASS

SABRE BASS

The Sabre Bass offers the professional player tremendous flexibility to suit individual playing styles, action characteristics, and string selections. Whether you prefer a fretted or fretless model, the Sabre Bass is meticulously crafted by hand with Music Man expertise. And each is registered, with the serial number stamped on the bridge. The instrument body is contoured to fit most players for greatest comfort. If the player takes a little time to learn how all the various controls work, he will obtain a variety of sounds not available on other instruments. With Music Man, you not only get your money's worth, you get a musical instrument of enduring quality.

SABRE BASS

THE NECK

Every part of a bass is important, but certainly the neck has the greatest impact on the feel and action of a fine instrument. From the tip of the headstock to the last fret, Music Man necks are designed to satisfy the needs of today's bass players.

HEADSTOCK, TUNING MACHINES AND NUT

The tuning machines are very high ratio for ease of use, with virtually no backlash. And they stay that way, thanks to self-tensioning and our case hardened, precision machined ferrules.

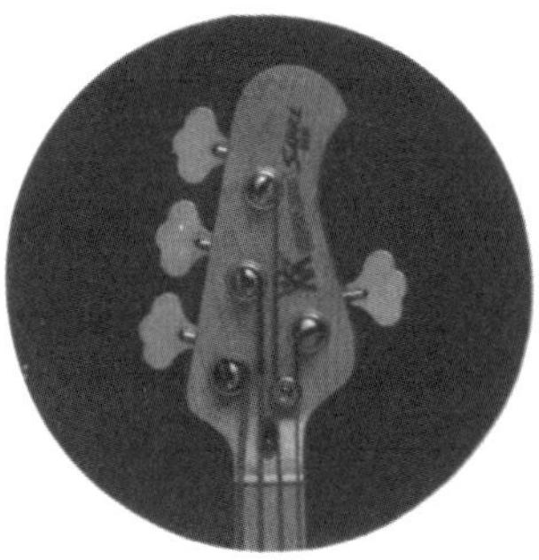

The neck and headstock are shaped so that the strings pull straight across the melamine nut, not at an angle. Our patented tapered string posts hold the strings close to the headstock and, on the top 2 strings, are assisted by a string

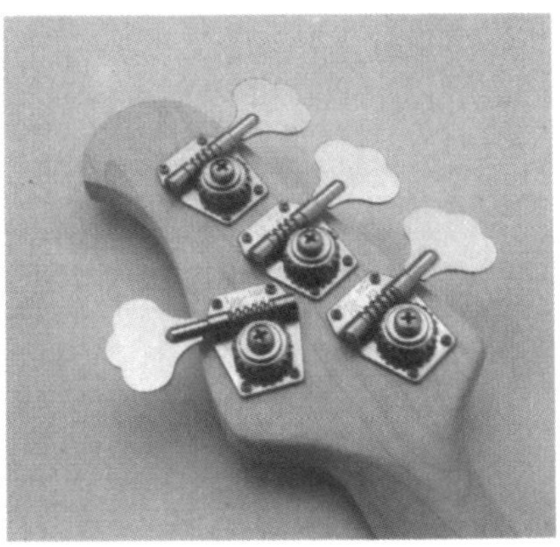

retainer. The retainer also shortens the effective string length between the nut and string post, reducing the tendency for unwanted sympathetic vibrations. By allowing extra wood thickness, we add plenty of strength to the critical junction of headstock and neck. This combination of design factors reduces the tendency for the instrument to go out of tune.

FRETBOARD AND FRETS

Whether you select the rosewood or maple fretboard, the scale length is 34", there are 21 jumbo frets, and the neck curvature radius is 7-1/2". (An ebony fretboard is standard on the fretless version.)

NECK CONSTRUCTION

As with all Music Man instruments, the neck and head are formed of a single piece of select, hard rock maple for strength, resistance to warp or twist, and sustain. The neck has a consistent, comfortable feel in any position. It is deeply seated where it joins the body, providing the optimum transfer of vibration between neck and body and increasing sustain. As with all Music Man guitars and basses, the neck tilt is screw adjustable.

THE BODY

The light weight, contoured, laminated ash or poplar body has a double cutaway that allows full access to all frets. Improved, deep-recess strap buttons provide positive grip on the strap and avoid enlarged strap holes for increased security. The body has been designed for maximum playing comfort.

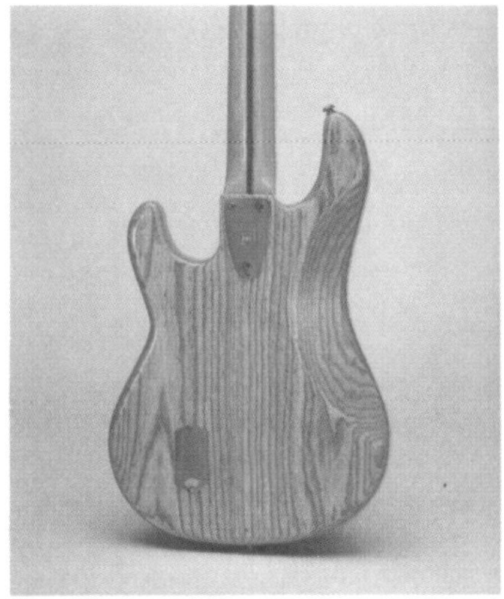

BRIDGE

The bridge is a heavy diecasting. The unique Music Man offset design allows the strings to pull through the lower end of the bridge casting, where they are offset to force the saddles against the bridge, resulting in a rigid, vibration-free assembly. String length and vertical height are fully adjustable with stainless steel bridge saddles. All screws are

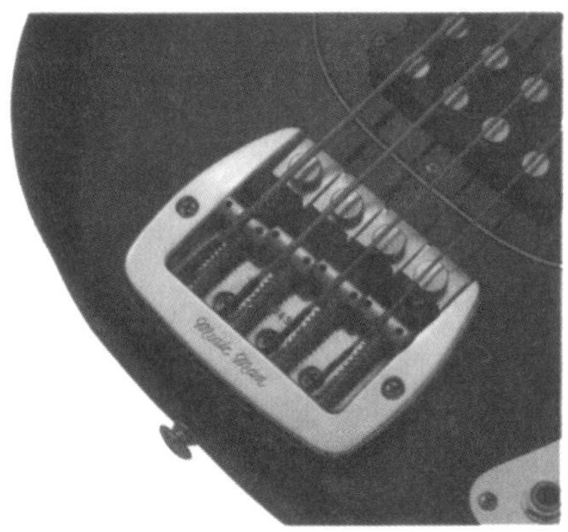

recessed within the saddle to avoid interference with picking or muting styles, and the entire bridge assembly is designed to eliminate jagged or rough edges. The bridge has an individual mute for each string, located just forward of the bridge saddles. Each is equipped with a thumb screw which adjusts the ten-

sion of the mute pad against the string. This allows you to change the degree of string damping to obtain different tonal characteristics.

PICKUPS

Two hum cancelling, high output, shielded pickups are precisely mounted for lead and rhythm sounds. The pickups are tri-mounted to give a full range of vertical and tilt adjustments.

PREAMP

The preamp's low impedance, high level output means you can plug directly into the mixing console and get the right sound whether recording or playing live.

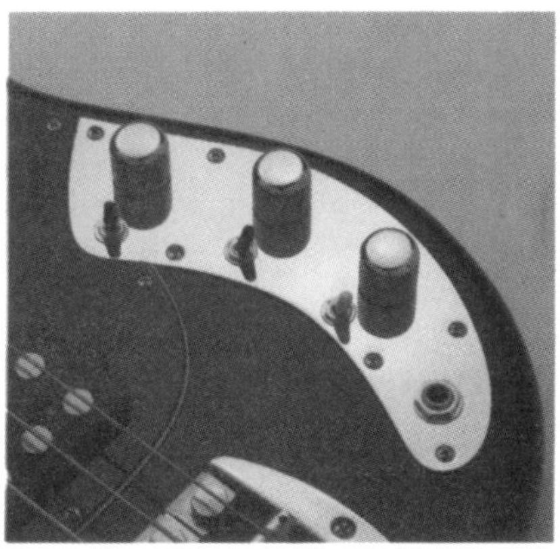

Without a preamp, equalization would be accomplished through passive filters which work by subtracting various ranges from the tonal spectrum. Because the Sabre Bass has a built-in preamp, its tone controls work on the principle of active equalization, which gives you the ability to subtract *and* boost these ranges.

SELECTOR SWITCH

The pickup selector switch allows you to choose between the lead and rhythm pickup, or to use them in combination.

PHASE SWITCH

Described simply, the phase switch puts the lead and rhythm pickups out of phase with one another so that a positive pulse from one is cancelled by a negative pulse from the other. This results in a thin, bright sound. The Sabre's phase switch works with the pickup selector in any position, so you can instantly get the sound you want.

BRIGHT SWITCH

The bright switch provides an instantaneous treble boost, and is useful for putting a subtle edge on the attack.

FINISH

A handsome, and durable lacquer finish is applied to the neck and body. You have a choice of finishes, all glossy unless otherwise noted: natural, *satin* finish natural, sunburst (a 3-color burst), walnut, white and black.

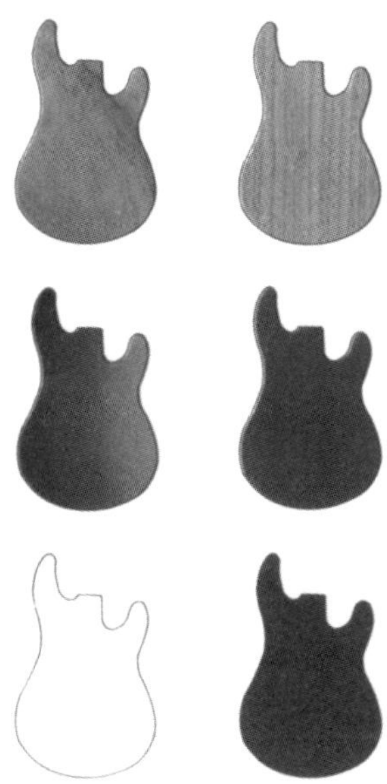

SABRE BASS SPECIFICATIONS

NUMBER OF FRETS:	21.
SCALE LENGTH:	34" (864 mm).
DIMENSIONS:	
OVERALL LENGTH	45" (1143 mm).
WIDTH AT WIDEST POINT	13" (330 mm).
OVERALL THICKNESS	neck .800" (20.3 mm), body 1-5/8" (41.3 mm).
PICKUPS:	2 anti-hum type.
OUTPUT:	+7 dBv (2.3 volts) maximum into 10 kohms or higher load. +2.5 dBv (1.36 volts RMS) into 600 ohms.
BATTERY:	9 V alkaline, MN-1604 Mallory or equivalent.
FRET MATERIAL:	Nickel silver alloy (18% Nickel is very hard for long wear).
FRETBOARD INLAY:	Dot style on face and side.
WOODS:	
NECK	Hard Rock Maple.
FRETBOARD	Maple or Rosewood (per customer request). Ebony standard on fretless models.
BODY	Ash or Poplar (depending on finish).
NECK CHARACTERISTICS:	7-1/2" (190 mm) fretboard radius.
FINISH:	High gloss lacquer (except as noted).
COLORS:	Natural, *satin* finish natural, sunburst, walnut, white, black.
HARDWARE:	All hardware heavy-duty chrome plated. Heavy-duty diecast bridge with stainless steel bridge saddles, individual string length adjustment and recessed saddle height adjustment screws. Tuning machines have patented tapered string post; 20:1 ratio and self-tensioning.

Replacement parts and service are available from your Music Man dealer. These specifications are subject to change without notice or obligation.

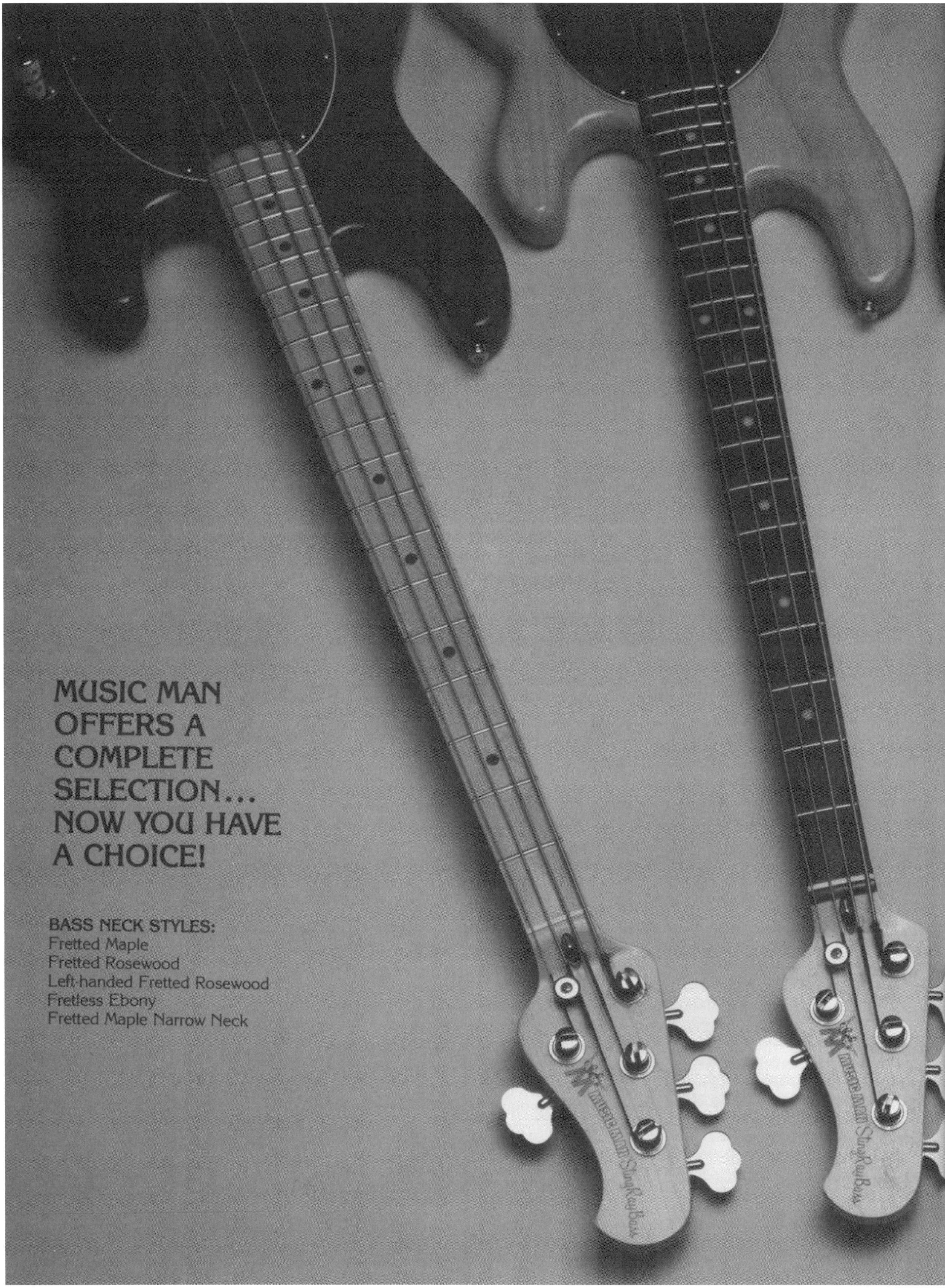
MUSIC MAN
OFFERS A
COMPLETE
SELECTION...
NOW YOU HAVE
A CHOICE!
BASS NECK STYLES:
Fretted Maple
Fretted Rosewood
Left-handed Fretted Rosewood
Fretless Ebony
Fretted Maple Narrow Neck

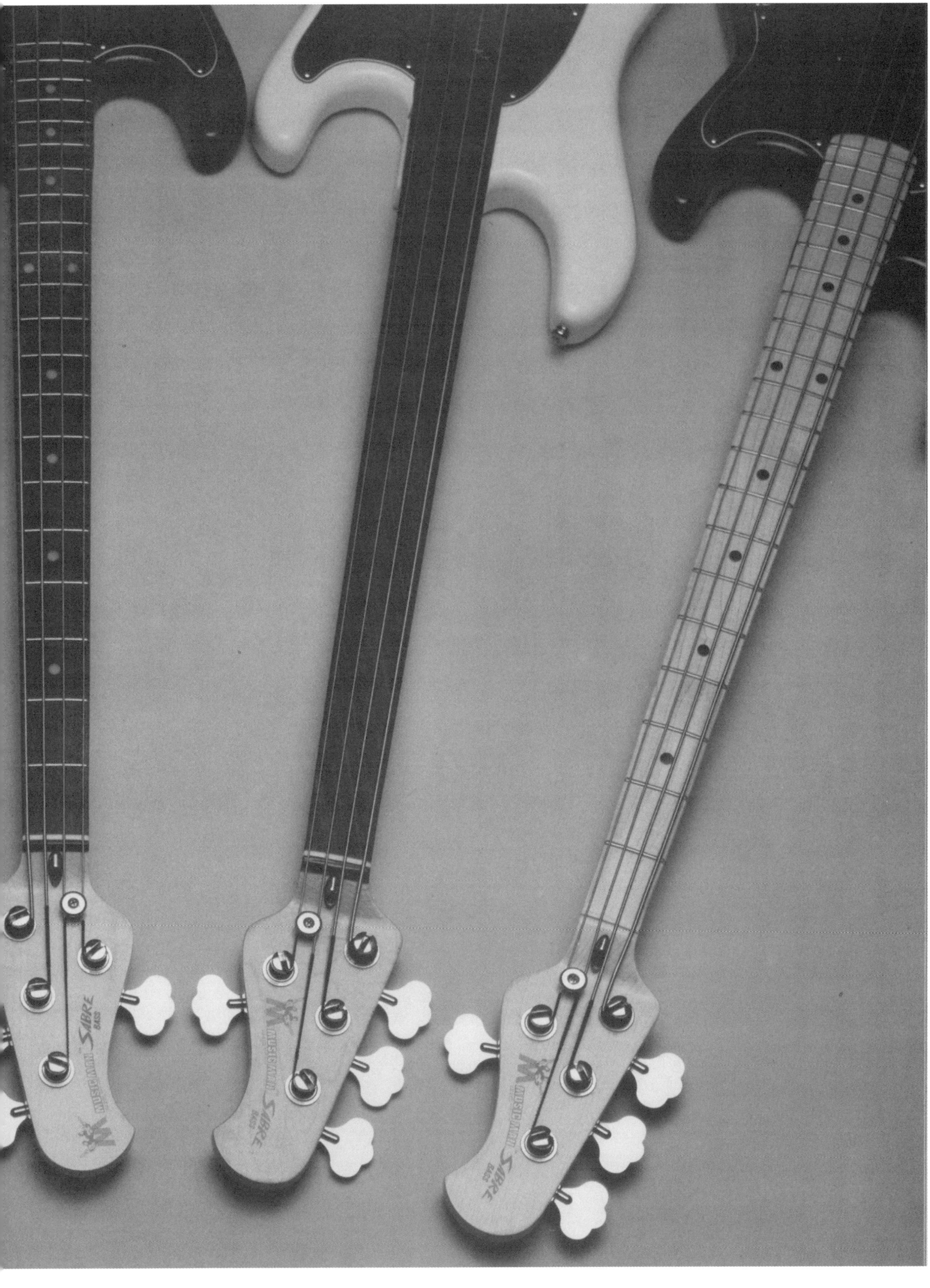
MUSIC MAN
SABRE
BASS

1
2
INPUT
VOLUME
TREBLE
BASS
1
2
BRIGHT
INPUT
NORMAL
VOLUME
MUSIC MAN

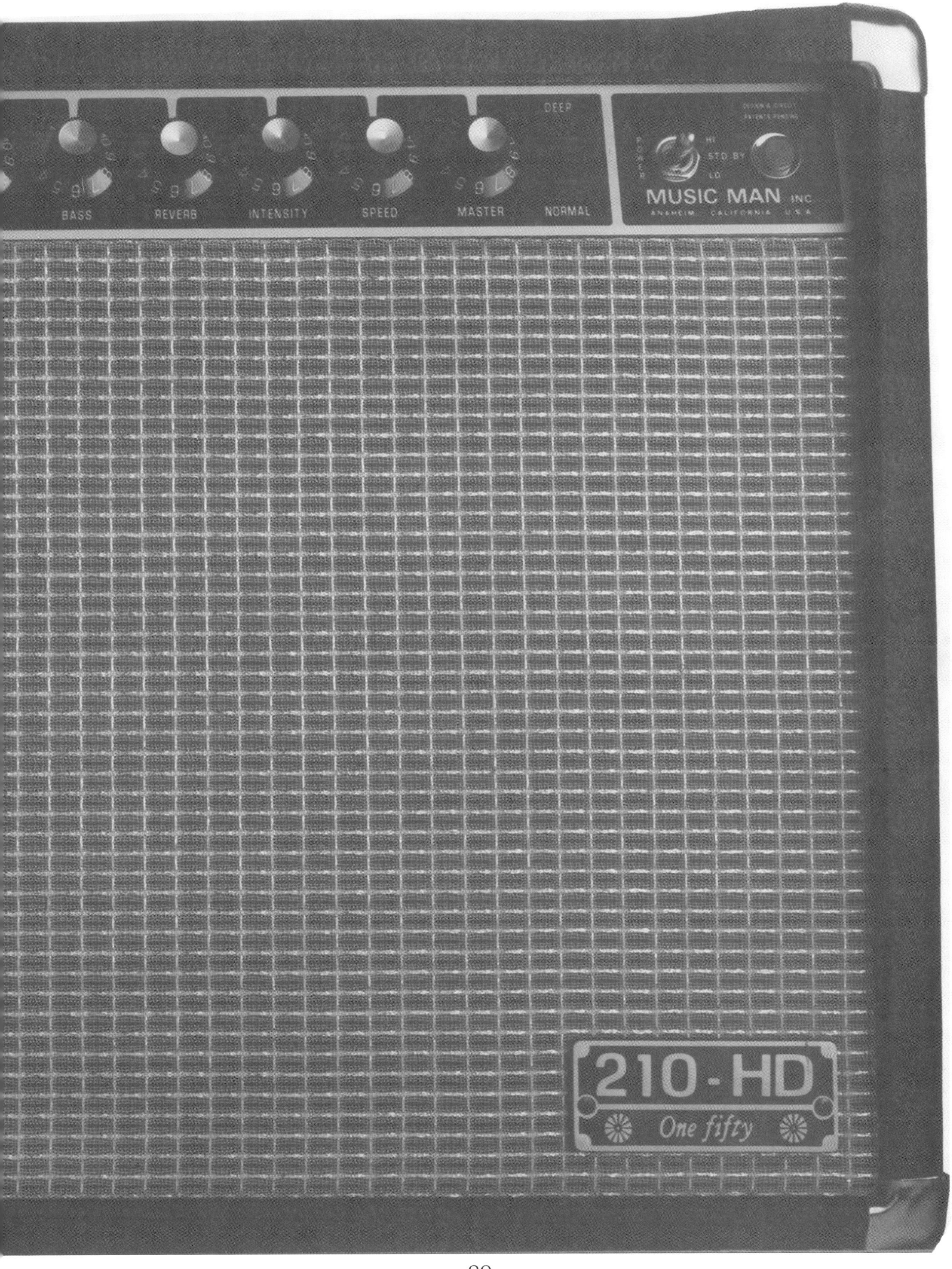
DEEP
BASS
REVERB
INTENSITY
SPEED
MASTER
NORMAL
POWER
HI
STD BY
LO
MUSIC MAN INC
ANAHEIM CALIFORNIA U.S.A
210-HD
One fifty

MUSIC MAN GUITAR & BASS AMPLIFIERS

The following pages present the most extensive line of musical instrument amplification systems we have ever produced. Recent trends toward smaller amplifiers have given birth to the new families of RP and RD models. A special welded steel chassis has been designed to allow a further reduction in size from the previous models. These are fully professional amplifiers, and are suitable for a variety of bandstand applications. The small size belies the power handling ability, which ranges from 65 to 100 watts RMS. The RP models provide reverb and a built-in phaser, while the RDs are equipped with two sets of gain controls and 2 volume controls which may be selected by a remote foot switch.

This arrangement allows the amplifiers to be switched between "clean" and any degree of sustain and distortion, and/or between any two desired volume settings. No longer is it necessary to compromise the gain of the amplifier to satisfy low noise performance while attempting to develop sufficient gain for good distortion. Consequently we can now offer an amplifier with outstanding distortion characteristics, reliable, compact, and with lots of flexibility.

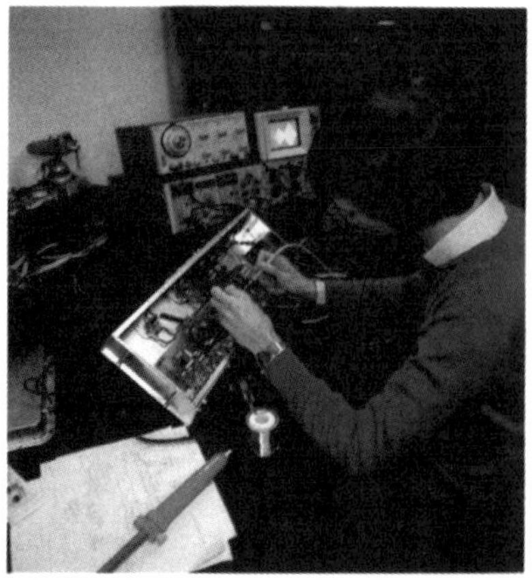

For those musicians who require two channels, we have redesigned the original 65 and 130 Series. These models have been given a 15% power boost to 75 and 150 watts respectively. While this does not yield an earthshaking increase in sound level, it does provide an extra margin of headroom for clean sound and greater dynamic range. The models which originally were equipped with tremolo now have a unique phaser circuit. The phaser is located *after* the preamplifier circuit, a design that virtually eliminates the whooshing noise which plagues all outboard phasers that go between the instrument and the amp. Another unusual feature is a pull switch on the phaser rate knob; the switch disables the sweep circuit, allowing the player to position the phase peaks and cancellations at any stationary point in the frequency spectrum. Some very interesting and unusual effects may be obtained in this manner, a bit like EQ, but not achievable with any normal tone controls.

A word about the pros and cons of vacuum tubes (valves) versus transistors seems appropriate. During the past decades, dozens of manufacturers have introduced transistor amplifiers (solid state) which were claimed to deliver a tube type sound. When compared side-by-side with true tube amps, none of the transistor units passed the acid test.

The main feature that brought the Music Man amplifier into prominence throughout the world is its hybrid design. The solid state front end provides the reliability and low noise performance that tubes could not deliver. However, the power stages that drive the speaker use vacuum tubes. This retains the warm and vibrant sound that transistors have so disappointingly failed to produce. Transistor amplifiers can be built for far less cost than tube amplifiers, but it has always been Music Man's policy to deliver the finest sound possible, not the cheapest.

In the remaining pages of this catalog, you will find a model that's suited to your own individual requirements. We urge you to visit your authorized Music Man dealer for a new experience in musical instrument amplification.

ELECTRONIC/CHASSIS FEATURE

- Most transistors and all integrated circuits are mounted in sockets

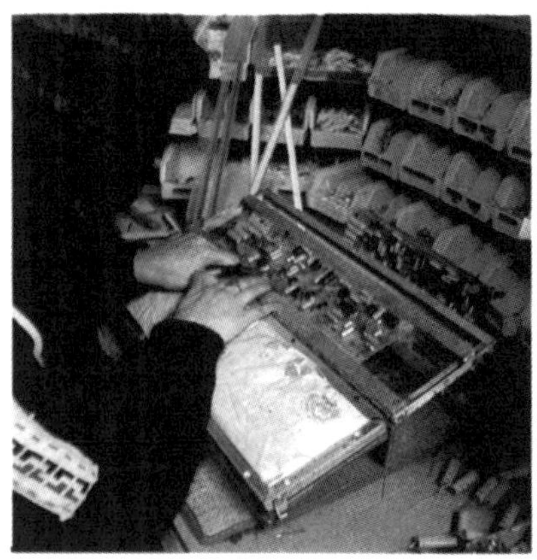

for serviceability. Exception — where mounting transistors directly to chassis affords better heat dissipation.

- Circuit boards are easily raised for access to the foil circuit traces.
- All wiring is high temperature (105° C) to withstand severe environments and long, hard use.

- Controls are connected to the circuit board with stranded wire leads to allow for easier service.
- Chassis is made of 18-gauge cold rolled steel, double plated to resist corrosion (first copper, then nickel).

- Die formed end bells are spot welded to the chassis in 22 places for extra strength.
- Special mounting brackets are used for heavy components such as the output transformer.
- Transformers are made with high-grade grain-oriented silicon steel laminations for extra efficiency.
- Components are conservatively rated for long life.

CABINET FEATURES

- Frame made from 3/4" Ponderosa Pine for extra strength and light weight.
- Rear panels made from 3/8" 5-ply plywood to guard against warping.
- Baffle board made from void-free marine plywood for strength.
- Lock joint construction provides 4 inches of glueing surface for each lineal inch of corner joint. No butt joints are used in the cabinet.
- Speakers are mounted with #8 machine screws and T-nuts. There are no dangerous studs to damage speaker cones.
- The Baffle board is surrounded by a 1/4" cleat to prevent grille cloth rattles.
- Collar washers are used under all wood screws to better distribute the load.
- All hardware is heavily plated for rust prevention.
- Case hardened metal fittings, made by Music Man, protect all 8 cabinet corners. The cabinet's distinctive styling protects the knobs and switches, too.

- A specially designed heavy-duty handle is secured by 4 #10 machine screws and T-nuts, so it won't twist, turn or pull loose.
- Amp glides are case hardened to prevent wear.
- All cabinets have built-in sockets for easy installation of optional heavy-duty casters. Each socket is mounted with 4 machine screws and T-nuts.
- Electro-magnetic screening is installed in the top of the cabinet to guard the chassis from interference and thus ensure noise-free amplifier operation.
- The heavy-duty vinyl covering material is felt backed for superior glueing, and hence longer wear.
- The specially woven grille cloth is more transparent to sound than conventional knits. It makes a difference.

MUSIC MAN CARES ABOUT DURABILITY, RELIABILITY AND QUALITY

The rugged physical construction of Music Man amplifiers guarantees durability that will protect your investment. We take the extra time and effort to do it right. For instance, all our cabinet hardware, including the chassis, glides, handles, etc., is made in house, where we can closely supervise the fabrication, hardening, plating, and finish.

Electronic parts are selected with ample reserve to accommodate a 10% voltage excursion without difficulty, so there is plenty of margin to avoid failure. Every chassis is tested, and the necessary adjustments made by a technician. After normal operation is certified, the amp is placed in a special test rack where it is driven to total overload for two minutes (during which it must dissipate twice its rated power), a test that is automatically repeated every 4 minutes for 4 hours. The amp is then re-tested and, only if still operating normally, is it assembled into its cabinet. The final test is done by a musician, not a meter. Only then is the unit permitted to be boxed for shipment.

MUSIC MAN SPEAKERS

To deliver the kind of top performance and sound quality a professional musician demands, Music Man has developed custom built speakers. Sure, speakers can be purchased out of a catalog, but not the kind of speakers needed to do the job right. Musical instrument speakers are unlike hi-fi, recording monitor or other speakers in that they are not used to reproduce a sound — they are used as part of the system which generates the original sound: an extension of the instrument itself which is essential in producing the desired tonality. Whereas speakers for recorded sound benefit from the limiting, compression, or other dynamic restrictions imposed by the tape machine and/or disc cutting process, musical instruments can punish a speaker with transients that are a thousand times more powerful than the average sound level. These speakers must withstand the abuse of touring, and the intense heat dissipated at high power levels. What's more, the speakers have to sound good to the discerning musician. Music Man speakers do their job well and they are tailored to the particular amplifier in which they are used.

All speakers, and especially instrument speakers, have a sound of their own. The theoretical "perfect" speaker with flat phase/amplitude response and no distortion whatsoever — if it could exist — would be a dismal flop as an instrument speaker. While thousands of loyal Music Man customers and their audiences enjoy the sound of our speakers, sound remains a matter of taste. For this reason, we also offer some of our systems with optional Electro-Voice EVM™ speakers. These popular sounding speakers had to pass rigorous tests before we certified them. Now that they've passed with flying colors, you have a choice of popular sounds — Music Man or Music Man/EVM.

SPEAKER SYSTEMS

Music Man single unit amplifier/speaker systems utilize open-back enclosures, popular for their light weight, excellent projection of upper harmonics, and broad dispersion of sound. Some musicians prefer to use separate speaker enclosures, for various reasons: they can be stacked for greater coverage or sound levels, they can "throw" the sound further, and they can provide greater efficiency.

To obtain higher sound levels one could simply use more speakers and amplifiers, or use larger amplifiers and speakers with higher power ratings, but the price would be high and portability would suffer greatly. What is needed instead is a more efficient speaker. Music Man RH Series speaker systems combine the best characteristics of two classic enclosure styles — bass reflex, with the speakers facing forward for good transient response, and a folded horn, for high efficiency. The RH Series (Reflex Horn) thus deliver more sound to the audience per watt of amplifier power, and they are still of reasonable dimensions for portability.

Another advantage of the RH design is that it delivers essentially the same sound to the performers on stage as to the audience, unlike some folded horns that require a great distance to fully develop the sound. Whereas the highs must bounce off internal surfaces in folded horns and W-boxes, the RH Series project harmonics directly, so the sound retains its definition and clarity. What's more, two RH Series speaker systems can be stacked with their drivers (speakers) next to each other, providing still greater acoustic efficiency due to the coupling effect between the units. These systems are enjoyed by guitarists, keyboard players, and bass players. (Bass players especially appreciate the RH Series because, to generate an equivalent listening volume, they would need twice the power for each octave lower in frequency — or twice the efficiency.

We also make two versions of a more traditional infinite baffle enclosure (large sealed box), the 412 B and the 412 GS, to satisfy the tonal preferences of some musicians.

SYLVANIA
MADE IN USA
6CA7
EL34
USA

THE RD SERIES

The Music Man RD Series guitar amplifiers combine state-of-the-art in vacuum tube design with a built-in reverb and foot-switchable distortion circuitry. Thanks to Music Man's many circuit refinements, you get the warm sound of tubes, plus cool running, low noise, and high power ratings.

The "R" in "RD Series" stands for "Reverb," and our built-in reverb has the new anti-shock "Z" spring delay, a genuine advantage over long springs when running high power. The reverb can be adjusted with a front panel control, and turned On and Off via a foot switch.

The "D" in "RD Series" stands for "Distortion." Five controls (two sets of Gain and Volume controls, and a footswitch that selects between them) let you dial in exactly the amount of this effect you want …from a clean well-defined sound, to a gentle warmth when you play hard, to an all-out raucus rock sound. You can adjust the Gain for more distortion, and then turn down the Volume to keep the power level where you want it. Thus, depending on how you set the controls, the footswitch selects between two different power levels, two different distortion levels at the same power, or a combination thereof. The footswitch has an indicator light so you know which set of controls is activated. The RD's also have a high power/standby/low power switch that is useful when you want to really push the tubes for the sound of a small amplifier being overdriven, yet not stress the speakers with full-power "squared" up sound. All units have provisions for an extension speaker.

The RD Series include a variety of features previously unobtainable in single units. A major improvement in flexibility and sound quality is provided by the RD's two line out/line in patch points, one for low and the other for higher levels. These jacks are handy for routing the pre-amplified sound to a pedal or studio-type effects device, then returning it to the amplifier. Inserting a volume

pedal at this jack point is the same as placing the Master Volume control on the floor; unlike pedals that come before the input, there is no need to increase the volume to compensate for loss, and when you turn down the level, you also turn down any background noise. The same Out/In jacks can be used to feed the power section of another RD or similar amp, making it easy to get double power, or more, above that which could be obtained from a single amplifier. Similarly, the output can be fed to a monitor, reinforcement or recording mixer.

Bright and Deep switches give instantaneous treble and bass boost. Their turnover frequencies are beyond the Bass, Middle and Treble controls, so you get the equivalent of 5-band equalization.

112RD-65

A 65 Watt RMS amplifier with a 12″ custom-built Music Man guitar speaker. Dimensions: 17″ H x 22-5/8″ L x 10-1/2″ W (430 mm x 575 mm x 265 mm). Weight: 47 lbs (21.4 kg)

RD-100

A 100 Watt RMS guitar amp head that may be used with most Music Man speaker systems. Dimensions: 8-1/2″ H x 22-5/8″ L x 8-1/2″ W (584 mm x 279 mm x 216 mm). Weight: 38 lbs (17.2 kg).

112RD-100EVM

A 100 Watt RMS amplifier and a 12″ heavy-duty Electro-Voice EVM™ speaker. Dimensions: 17″ H x 22-5/8″ L x 10-1/2″ W (430 mm x 575 mm x 265 mm). Weight: 57 lbs (25.9 kg).

210RD-100

A 100 Watt RMS amplifier and two 10″ custom-built Music Man guitar speakers. Dimensions: 15-1/8″ H x 22-5/8″ L x 10-1/2″ W (584 mm x 406 mm x 267 mm). Weight: 55 lbs (25 kg).

115RD-100EVM

A 100 Watt RMS amplifier and a 15″ heavy-duty Electro-Voice EVM™ speaker. Dimensions: 19-3/4″ H x 22-5/8″ L x 10-7/16″ W (500 mm x 575 mm x 265 mm). Weight: 72 lbs (32.7 kg).

THE RP SERIES

The Music Man RP Series guitar amplifiers combine the state-of-the-art in vacuum tube design with built-in foot-switchable phaser and reverb, plus adjustable distortion circuitry. Thanks to Music Man's many circuit refinements, you get the warm sound of tubes, plus cool running, low noise, and high power ratings.

The "R" in "RP Series" stands for "Reverb." The built-in reverb has the same new anti-shock "Z" spring delay, front panel control and foot-switch capability as the RD series.

The "P" in "RP Series" stands for "Phaser." Our built-in foot-switchable unit is superior to external units because it operates on a preamplified signal, so there is little "swishing" of background noise, just the desired phase effect.

Bright and Deep switches yield instantaneous treble and bass boost, and their turnover frequencies are beyond the Bass, Middle and Treble controls, so you get the equivalent of 5-band equalization.

The RP Series will give you the same range of sounds as the RD Series, depending on how you set the Gain and Volume controls. You adjust the Gain up and down for more or less distortion, and then adjust the Volume for the desired power level. And the RP's also have a high power/standby/Low power switch for getting the sound of a small overdriven amplifier without overstressing the speakers.

The RP Series include a variety of features previously unobtainable in single units. Like the RD Series, they have low and high level line out/line in patch points which avoid noise and improve performance with all kinds of effects units, and facilitate interface with other amps and mixing consoles.

112RP-65

A 65 Watt RMS amplifier with a 12″ custom-built Music Man guitar speaker. Dimensions: 17″ H x 22-5/8″ L x 10-1/2″ W (430 mm x 575 mm x 265 mm). Weight: 47 lbs (21.4 kg)

RP-100

A 100 Watt RMS guitar amp head that may be used with all Music Man speaker systems. Dimensions: 8-1/2″ H x 22-5/8 L x 8-1/2 W (584 mm x 279 mm x 216 mm). Weight: 37 lbs (16.8 kg).

112RP-100EVM

A 100 Watt RMS amplifier and a 12″ heavy-duty Electro-Voice EVM™ speaker. Dimensions: 17″ H x 22-5/8″ L x 10-1/2″ W (430 mm x 575 mm x 265 mm). Weight: 57 lbs (25.9 kg).

210RP-100

A 100 Watt RMS amplifier and two 10″ custom-built Music Man guitar speakers. Dimensions: 15-1/8″ H x 22-5/8″ L x 10-1/2″ W (584 mm x 406 mm x 267 mm). Weight: 55 lbs (25 kg).

115RP-100EVM

A 100 Watt RMS amplifier and a 15″ heavy-duty Electro-Voice EVM™ speaker. Dimensions: 19-3/4″ H x 22-5/8″ L x 10-7/16″ W(500 mm x 575 mm x 265 mm). Weight: 67 lbs (30 kg).

AMPLIFIER FRONT PANEL

RD

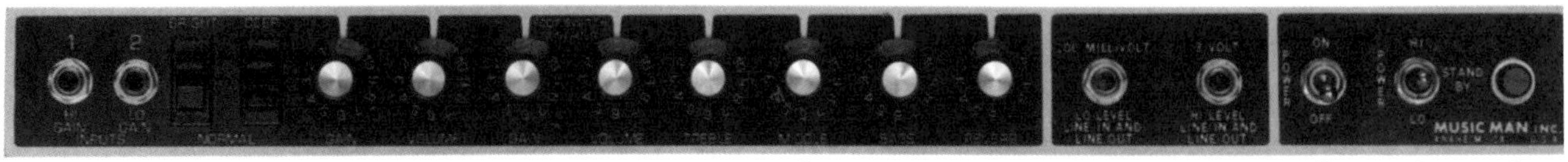

A B C D E L M N F G H I Q R S

A. INPUT JACK 1
Standard phone jack instrument input. Has more gain than Input Jack 2. Useful for low output pick-ups, or for easier overdrive of the amplifier.

B. INPUT JACK 2
Standard phone jack instrument input. Has 6 dB less gain (half the level) of Input Jack 1. Useful for clean sound with high output pick-ups. If Jacks 1 and 2 are both used simultaneously, they both have the same sensitivity.

C. BRIGHT SWITCH
Rocker switch provides instantaneous treble boost. Has a higher turnover frequency than the treble tone control, and can be used together for additional bite. By enhancing upper harmonics, Bright can lend brilliance to an otherwise dull sounding instrument. On the 75- and 150- Series, the Bright control is designed specifically for adding sparkle at low volume levels.

D. DEEP SWITCH
The deep switch provides insta taneous bass boost for a warmer sound at low volume levels. Has lower turnover frequency than th bass tone control on RD and RP series. On two channel models, t deep switch is a high pass filter (HPF) which attenuates all freque cies below 100Hz. at a 6dB/OCT slope when in the normal positio The high pass filter (HPF) is bypassed when the switch is in the deep position.

RP

A B C D E F G H I J K L Q R S

E. GAIN CONTROL (Labeled VOLUME on 75 & 150 Series)
Adjusts the amount of amplification that occurs immediately after the input jack. If the amplification is increased here (higher gain), successive circuits can be more easily overdriven for more distortion. Cleaner sound is achieved at lower gain settings; if a louder output is needed at the speaker, the Volume control can then be turned up (Master on 75 or 150 amp).

F. TREBLE CONTROL
This tone (Equalizer) control adjusts the amount of boost (accentuation) or cut (attenuation) in the high frequency range.

G. MIDDLE CONTROL
This tone control adjusts the amount of boost or cut in the middle of the frequency spectrum.

H. BASS CONTROL
This tone control adjusts the amount of boost or cut in the low frequency range.

I. REVERB CONTROL
Adjusts the amount of reverb (spri delayed sound) that is mixed together with the direct-from-the-instrument sound. Reverb adds fullness to the sound, and lessen the presence.

J. PHASOR (INTENSITY) CONTR
Sets the amount of phaser effect from no phasing, to a slight tremolo-like wavering, to very de filter notches.

75/150

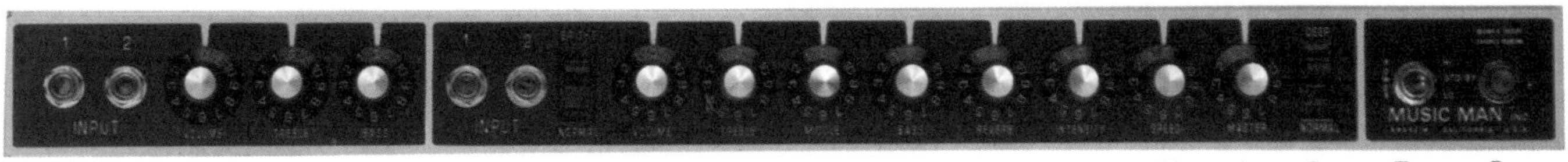

A B E F H O P C E F G H I J K L D R S

K. PHASOR RATE (SPEED) CONTROL
Sets the speed of the phasor sweep from very slow to very fast. Available only on the 75 and 150 series, the automatic sweep turns OFF when the knob is pulled out, and you can rotate the control to manually set the phasor filters where you want them.

L. MASTER VOLUME CONTROL
Sets the level in the final stage of the preamplifier circuitry just ahead of the power amplifier. Volume is essentially independent of the Gain settings; if Gain is turned up for more distortion, also increasing the level, Volume can be set for any desired power level. On the two-channel 75- and 150-Series amps, Master Volume adjusts the level from all inputs.

M. FOOTSWITCH-ACTUATED GAIN CONTROL
On the RD Series amps, this control serves the same purpose as the other Gain control; a footswitch alternates between the two controls for instant selection of different distortion levels.

N. FOOTSWITCH-ACTUATED VOLUME CONTROL
On the RD Series amps, this control serves the same purpose as the other Volume control; the same footswitch that selects which Gain control is active simultaneously selects which Volume control is active.

75/150

A B C E F G H O P C E F G H I J K L D R S

O. CHANNEL 2 INPUT JACK 1
A high gain (high sensitivity) input jack for the amplifier's second input channel. Works just like Input Jack 1 on channel 1.

P. CHANNEL 2 INPUT JACK 2
A low gain (low sensitivity) input jack for the amplifier's second input channel. Works just like Input Jack 2 on channel 1; when both channel 2 jacks are used, they have the same sensitivity.

Q. POWER ON/OFF SWITCH
(On rear panel of 75 & 150 series)
Turns AC power ON and OFF. When the switch is OFF, the amplifier is completely shut down.

R. POWER SELECTOR SWITCH (HI/STANDBY/LO)
In Standby position, tubes are kept warm and the preamp works, but high voltage is not applied to the tube plates, so there is no power fed to the speakers. In Hi position, the tubes are fed full plate voltage and the amplifier can develop its rated output power. In Lo position, voltage to the tube plates is reduced; you get the same sound quality, but at half the power, so there is less chance of blowing a speaker when using maximum distortion, and big-amp sound can be obtained at somewhat lower volume levels for studio work.

S. POWER INDICATOR LIGHT
A red indicator lamp is illuminated whenever the Power switch is ON, regardless of the Power Selector Switch position.

THE 75 SERIES

The Music Man 75 Series is a line of moderate power state-of-the-art vacuum tube guitar amplifiers which feature two input channels, built-in foot-switchable reverb and phaser, and 75 Watts RMS of cool, low-noise, penetrating power.

Channel 1 is equipped with a pair of input jacks, a Volume (input gain) control, and Bass, and Treble EQ controls; some 75 Series models also include a Middle EQ control and a Bright switch. Channel 2 has the full complement of channel 1 features plus Reverb and Phasor controls. The Deep switch and Master level control affects both channels' sound.

The built-in reverb has a long spring delay. The reverb is adjusted with a front panel control, and turned On and Off via a footswitch.

Bright and Deep switches provide an instantaneous treble and bass boost, and have turnover frequencies differing from the tone controls, thus adding to the available EQ effects.

You can adjust the Volume for more or less distortion, then adjust the Master control for the desired output level. You thus obtain any desired tonality from gentle warmth to an all-out raucus rock sound.

A single player can plug two instruments into the amp, and set just the right EQ and level for each instrument — a really fast and convenient way to switch instruments in the middle of a show.

Our built-in phaser operates on a preamplified signal, so there is little "swishing" of background noise, just the desired phase effect. What's more, the Speed control can be pulled out to stop the sweep, allowing the phaser to be manually set at unique filter positions for sounds you could never achieve with a conventional EQ circuit.

The input Volume controls can be adjusted for relative balance and more or less warmth or distortion; the Master control and high/standby/low power switch then set the desired output level.

75R

A 75 Watt RMS guitar amp head with 2 input-channels. Suitable for use with most Music Man speaker systems. Dimensions: 11" H x 24-7/16" L x 9-15/16" W. Weight: 40 lbs (18.14 kg).

112-75

A 75 Watt RMS amplifier with 2 input channels and a single 12" custom-built Music-Man guitar speaker in an open back cabinet. Dimensions: 17" H x 24-7/16" L x 10-7/16 W (622 mm x 686 x 267 mm). Weight: 50 lbs (22.7 kg).

210-75

A 75 Watt RMS amplifier with 2 input channels and two 10" custom-built Music Man guitar speakers in an open back cabinet. Dimensions: 15" H x 24-7/16" L x 10-7/16" W (622 mm x 381 mm x 267 mm). Weight 53 lbs (24 kg).

212-75

A 75 Watt RMS amplifier with 2 input channels, including a Bright switch and Middle EQ control on channel 1. The amp has two custom-built 12" Music Man guitar speakers in an open back cabinet. Dimensions: 19-7/16" H x 26-7/16" L x 10-15/16 W (673 mm x 495 mm x 279 mm). Weight: 60 lbs. (27.3 kg).

410-75

A 75 Watt RMS amplifier with 2 input channels, and 4 10" custom-built Music Man guitar speakers in an open-back cabinet. Dimensions: 25-1/2" H x 24-7/16" L x 10-15/16" W (622 mm x 648 mm x 279 mm). Weight: 72 lbs. (32.7 kg).

THE 150 SERIES

The Music Man 150 Series is a line of high-power state-of-the-art vacuum tube guitar amplifiers which feature two input channels, built-in foot-switchable reverb and phaser, and 150 Watts RMS of penetrating power to put your sound up front.

Channel 1 is equipped with a pair of input jacks, a Volume (input gain) control, and Bass, and Treble EQ controls; some models also include a Middle EQ control and a Bright switch. Channel 2 has the full complement of channel 1 features plus Reverb and Phaser controls. The Deep switch and Master level control affect both channels at once.

The built-in foot-switchable reverb has a long spring delay and can be adjusted with a front panel control.

Bright and Deep switches provide an instantaneous treble and bass boost, and since their turnover frequencies are different from those of the tone controls, the overall choice of sounds is greatly enhanced.

You can adjust the Volume for more or less distortion, then adjust the Master control for the desired output level. You thus obtain any desired tonality from gentle warmth to an all-out raucus rock sound.

Like the 75 Series, the built-in low-noise phaser can be manually adjusted or set for continuous automatic sweep, for unique sounds unavailable with any conventional EQ or phaser.

A High power/Standby/Low power switch is invaluable when you want to really push the tubes for the sound of a small amplifier being overdriven, yet not stress the speakers with full-power "squared" up sound.

HD-150R
A 150Watt RMS guitar amp head with 2 input-channels. Suitable for use with most Music Man speaker systems. Dimensions: 11″ H x 24-7/16″ L x 9-15/16″ W. Weight: 40 lbs (18.14 kg).

210HD-150
A 150 Watt RMS amplifier with 2 input channels, and two 10″ custom-built Music Man guitar speakers in an open back cabinet. Dimensions: 15″ H x 24-7/16″ L x 10-7/16″ W (673 mm x 495 mm x 279 mm). Weight: 57 lbs (25.9 kg).

212HD-150
A 150 Watt RMS amplifier with 2 input channels, including a Bright switch and Middle EQ control on channel 1. The amp has two 12″ custom-built Music Man guitar speakers in an open back cabinet. Dimensions: 26-1/2″ W x 19-1/2″ H x 11″ D (673 mm x 495 mm x 279 mm). Weight: 72 lbs (32.7 kg).

212HD-150 EVM
Almost identical to the 212HD-150, but uses two heavy-duty 12″ Electro-Voice EVM™ speakers. Weight: 92 lbs (41.72 kg).

410HD-150
A 150 Watt RMS amplifier with 2 input channels and 4 10″ custom-built Music Man guitar speakers in an open back cabinet. Dimensions: 25-1/2″ H x 24-7/16″ L x 10-15/16″ W (622 mm x 648 mm x 279 mm). Weight: 75 lbs (34 kg).

115HD-150-EVM
A 150 Watt RMS amplifier with 2 input channels and a single 15″ heavy-duty Electro-Voice EVM™ speaker in an open back cabinet. Dimensions: 20-1/2″ H x 24-7/16″ L x 10-15/16″ W (621 mm x 522 mm x 278 mm). Weight: 76 lbs (33.7 kg).

AMPLIFIER SPECIFICATIONS

		RD SERIES	RP SERIES	TWO CHANNEL SERIES	
POWER OUTPUT DELIVERED TO 4 OR 8 OHM SPEAKERS		All -100 models, 100 watts RMS All -65 models, 65 watts RMS		All -75 models 75 watts RMS	All -150 models 150 watts RMS
INDIVIDUAL MODELS (Followed by speaker quantity, type and nominal diameter, except as noted for head-only models)		RD-100 (Head)	RP-100 (Head)	75* (Bass Head)	HD-150* (Bass Head)
		112-RD65 1 Music Man 12″	112-RP65 1 Music Man 12″	75R (Head)	HD-150R (Head)
		112-RD100-EVM 1 EVM 12″	112-RP100-EVM 1 EVM 12″	112-75 1 Music Man 12″	115-HD150-EVM 1 EVM 15″
		115-RD100-EVM 1 EVM 15″	115-RP100-EVM 1 EVM 15″	210-75 2 Music Man 10″	210-HD150 2 Music Man 10″
		210-RD100 2 Music Man 10″	210-RP100 2 Music Man 10″	212-75 2 Music Man 12″	212-HD150 2 Music Man 12″
				410-75 4 Music Man 10″	212-HD150-EVM 2 EVM 12″
					410-HD150 4 Music Man 10″
MINIMUM INPUT SENSITIVITY	Input 1 Input 2	0.9 mV 2.2 mV	0.9 mV 2.1 mV	1 mV 2 mV	1 mV 2 mV
INPUT IMPEDANCE	Input 1 Input 2	215,000 ohms 122,000 ohms	215,000 ohms 122,000 ohms	215,000 ohms 122,000 ohms	215,000 ohms 122,000 ohms
TONE CONTROL CENTER FREQUENCIES	Treble Middle Bass	3.3 Hz 460 Hz 65 Hz	3.3 kHz 460 Hz 65 Hz	3.3 kHz 460 Hz* 65 Hz*	3.3 kHz 460 Hz* 65 Hz*
BRIGHT SWITCH BOOST		+15 dB @3.2 kHz	+15 dB @3.2 kHz	+15 dB @3.2 kHz	+15 db @3.2 kHz
DEEP SWITCH BOOST		+13 dB @54 Hz	+13 dB @54 Hz	Turnover @100 Hz 6 dB/OCT HPF.	Turnover @100 Hz 6 dB/OCT HPF.
LOW LEVEL LINE IN/OUT JACK	Nom. Level Output Z Input Z	0.1 volts RMS < 700 ohms > 180 kohms	0.1 volts RMS < 700 ohms > 180 kohms	Not Applicable	Not Applicable
HIGH LEVEL LINE IN/OUT JACK	Nom. Level Output Z Input Z	3 volts RMS < 700 ohms > 180 kohms	3 volts RMS < 700 ohms > 180 kohms	Not Applicable	Not Applicable
PHASER RATE		Not Applicable	0.05 Hz - 8 Hz	0.05 Hz - 8 Hz*	0.05 Hz - 8 Hz*
REVERB		Footswitchable	Footswitchable	Footswitchable*	Footswitchable*
POWER REQUIREMENTS ±		120 V AC, 60 Hz	120 V AC, 60 Hz	120 V AC, 60 Hz	120 V AC, 60 Hz
3 AG FUSE RATING		3 amp	3 amp	5 amp	5 amp
NOTES:		2 Gain & 2 Volume controls, foot-switch selectable	Footswitchable 4 stage phaser	Footswitchable 4 stage phaser	Footswitchable 4 stage phaser

*Models 75 and HD-150 Bass Heads: Middle and Bass tone control turnover frequencies differ on the two bass channels (Mid=325 Hz, Bass=32 Hz), and reverb and phaser is not provided.

BASS HEADS

75

A 75 Watt RMS bass amp head with 2 input channels. Channel 1 (the "Normal" channel) includes High and Low gain Input jacks, a Volume (gain) control, a Bright switch, and Bass, Middle and Treble EQ controls. Channel 2 (the "Bass" channel) includes all the controls of channel 1 plus a Deep switch and a Master volume control for both channels. Channel 1 is used for most bass instruments (it is marked "Normal"), and provides the maximum bass response. The channel 2 Bass tone control is modified for less overall bass response, an aid when using very bass-heavy instruments (hence the channel designation "Bass"). The unit is Suitable for use with most Music Man speaker systems. Dimensions: 8-1/2" H x 22-11/16" L x 9-15/16" W. Weight: 34 lbs. (15.4 kg).

HD-150

A 150 Watt RMS bass amp head with controls and features identical to those of the 75 head. Suitable for use with most Music Man speaker systems. Dimensions: 8-1/2" H x 22-11/16" L x 9-15/16" W. Weight: 40 lbs. (18.14 kg).

ENCLOSURE SPECIFICATIONS

CABINET	INCHES O.D. H x L x W	CENTIMETERS O.D. H x L x W	WEIGHT LBS	WEIGHT KILOS	SPEAKER COMPLIMENT	Enclosure Impedance	Power Capability (RMS)
115RH-75	27-3/8 x 27-3/8 x 12-15/16	69.933 x 69.533 x 32.861	60	132.3	1 — 15" Music Man	8 ohms	75 watts
115RH-150 EVM	27-3/8 x 27-3/8 x 12-15/16	69.933 x 69.533 x 32.861	70	154.35	1 — 15" Electro-Voice	8 ohms	150 watts
118RH-150 EVM	31-7/8 x 27-3/8 x 16-1/2	80.963 x 69.533 x 41.91	94	207.27	1 — 18" Electro-Voice	8 ohms	150 watts
210RH-150	22-3/8 x 26-3/8 x 12-15/16	56.833 x 26.375 x 32.861	52	114.66	2 — 10" Music Man	4 ohms	150 watts
212RH-150	27-3/8 x 27-3/8 x 12-15/16	69.533 x 69.533 x 32.861	69	152.145	2 — 12" Music Man	4 ohms	150 watts
212RH-150 EVM	27-3/8 x 27-3/8 x 12-15/16	69.533 x 69.533 x 32.861	89	196.245	2 — 12" Electro-Voice	4 ohms	150 watts
412B	27-3/8 x 27-3/8 x 16-1/2	69.533 x 69.533 x 41.91	82	180.81	4 — 12" Music Man	8 ohms	150 watts
412GS	27-3/8 x 27-3/8 x 12-15/16	69.533 x 69.533 x 32.861	78	171.99	4 — 12" Music Man	8 ohms	150 watts
210S	29-1/4 x 13-1/4 x 10-15/16	74.295 x 33.655 x 27.781	42	92.61	2 — 10" Music Man 1 — PE120 Motorola 2000Hz horn	4 ohms	75 watts
12M-1	15-7/8 x 20-1/8 x 11-1/2	40.323 x 51.118 x 28.252	28	61.74	1 — 12" Music Man 1 — PE120 Motorola 2000Hz horn	8 ohms	75 watts
12M-1 EVM	15-7/8 x 20-1/8 x 11-1/2	40.323 x 51.118 x 28.252	42	92.61	1 — 12" Electro-Voice 1 — PE120 Motorola 2000Hz horn	8 ohms	100 watts

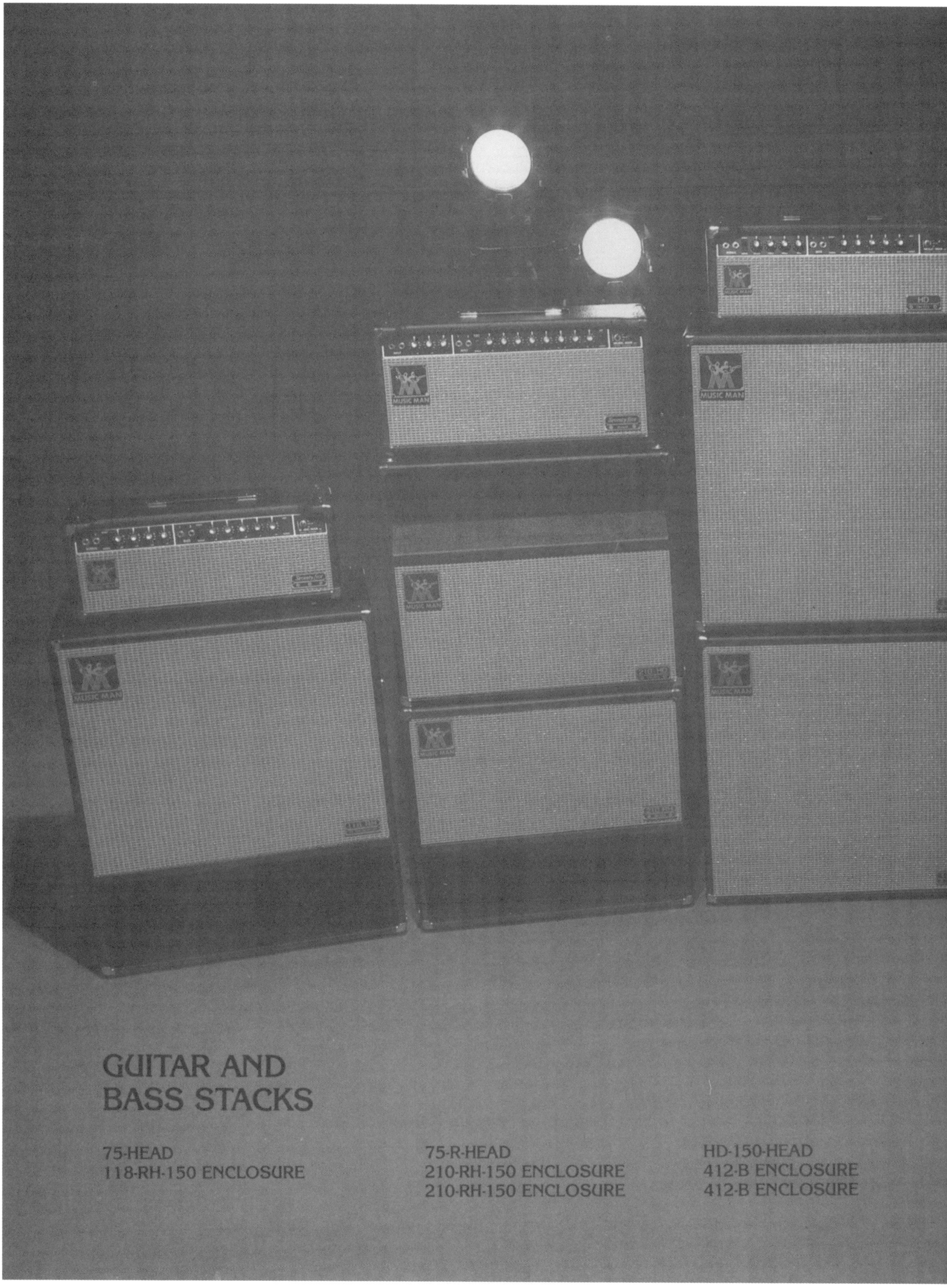

GUITAR AND BASS STACKS

75-HEAD
118-RH-150 ENCLOSURE

75-R-HEAD
210-RH-150 ENCLOSURE
210-RH-150 ENCLOSURE

HD-150-HEAD
412-B ENCLOSURE
412-B ENCLOSURE

HD-150
MUSIC MAN
HD-150R-HEAD
412-GS ENCLOSURE
412-GS ENCLOSURE
100-RD-HEAD
212-RH-150 ENCLOSURE
212-RH-150 ENCLOSURE
100-RP-HEAD
115-RH-75 ENCLOSURE

ACCESSORIES

Amp casters, set of 4
Amp corners, set of 4
Amp glides, set of 4
Amp handle
Allen wrenches — guitar
  set/bass set
Ball casters, set of 4
Bass bag — black, brown
Guitar bag — black, brown
Bone nuts
ABS bass case
Control knobs, set of 3
Cabinet mount — one 9", one 12",
  one 15"
Straight cord, 12 each
Guitar polish, 1 box
Guitar slide — small, medium,
  large
Picks — Sideman MM351 light,
    medium, heavy
  Jazz MM354 light,
    medium, heavy
  Small Jazz MM358 light,
    medium, heavy
Bass machine heads, 1 set of 4
Guitar machine heads, 1 set of 6
Polish cloth (wood)
Polish cloth (metal)
Screwdriver (flat)
Screwdriver (phillips)
'T' shirt — black, navy, light blue
Golf shirt — blue, black
Pocket shirt — blue
Canvas shoulder bag (tote bag)
Stacking kit
Strap button
3½" leather strap — black,
  natural, mustard, brown
2½" leather strap — black,
  natural, mustard, brown
Woven straps, assorted colors
String cutters
String winder
Tuning fork 922A
Tuning fork 924A
Wheelies, set of 4
Wrist bags
String kit
Bass string kit
String sets — 008 ex-1
  009 super 011 light
  010 regular 013 medium
Bass string sets —
  round wound
  flat wound
  polished round wound, light
  polished round wound, medium

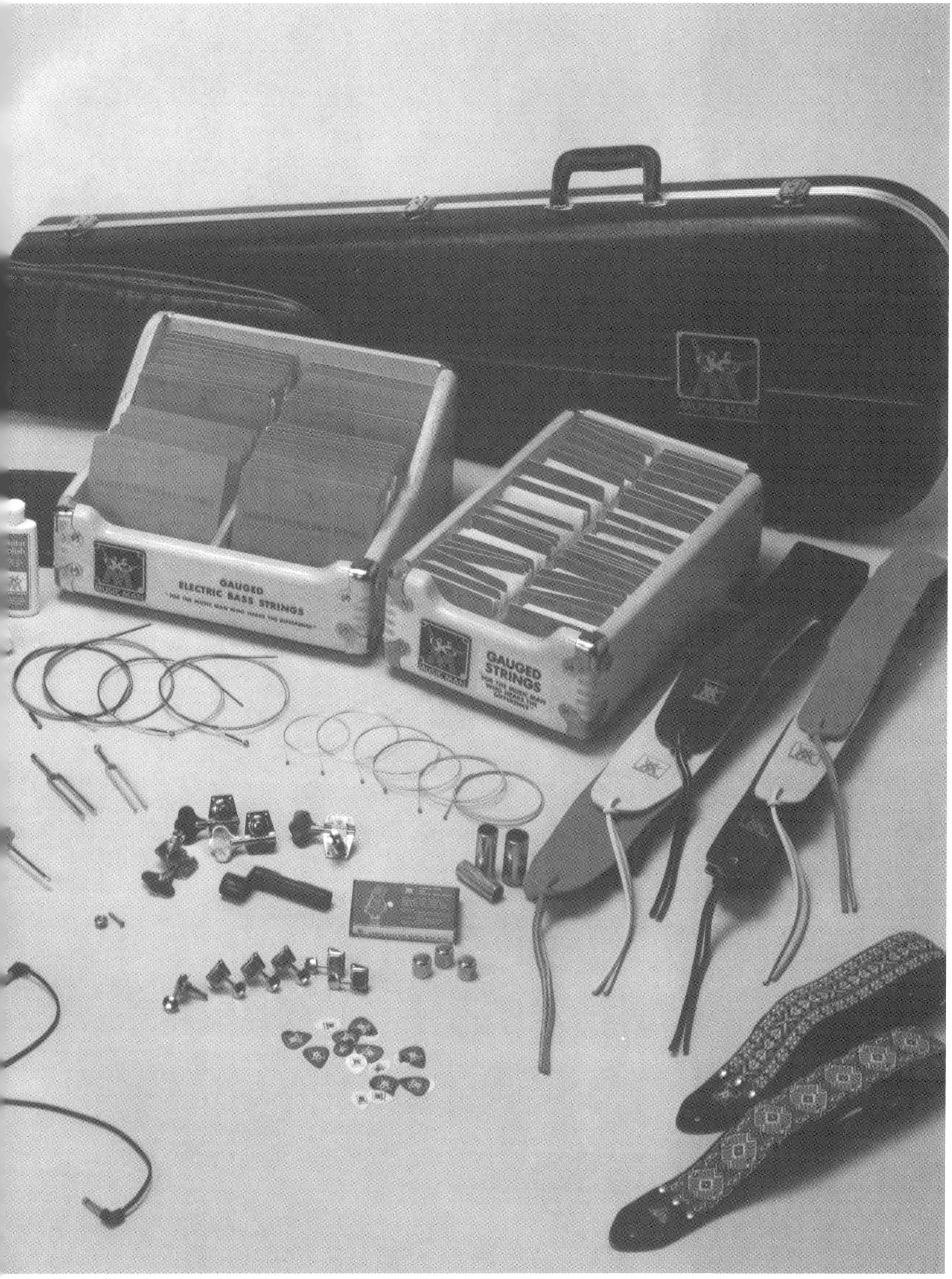
MUSIC MAN
GAUGED
ELECTRIC BASS STRINGS
"FOR THE MUSIC MAN WHO HEARS THE DIFFERENCE"
MUSIC MAN
GAUGED
STRINGS
"FOR THE MUSIC MAN
WHO HEARS THE
DIFFERENCE"
MUSIC MAN

BACKING THE BEST...

DOMESTIC
Aerosmith
Loren Balman
Paul Barrere/Little Feat
Bee Jay Recording Studios,
  Orlando, Florida
Glen Campbell
Eric Clapton
Thumbs Carllile
Gene Cotton
Joel Di Bartolo/Doc Severinson
Don Everly
Donna Fargo
Freebo/Bonnie Raitt
Leon Gaer
Crystal Gayle
Bill Graham
Sal Guglielmi/Donna Summer
Emmy Lou Harris
Charlie Harrison/Poco
Louis Johnson/The
  Brothers Johnson
Albert Lee
Neil Levang/Lawrence Welk
Mike Hamilton/Kenny Loggins
David Margen/Santana
Kevin McCormick/Brooklyn Dreams
Mother's Finest
Mayf Nutter
Oak Ridge Boys
Palomino Club
Dolly Parton
Alvino Rey
Michael Rodriguez/Cheek
Dann Rogers
Kenny Rogers
Chico Ryan/Sha Na Na
Tennessee Three/Johnny Cash
Dottie West
Johnny Winter Group
Jimmy Wyble
Lloyd Ellis/Pete Fountain

INTERNATIONAL
Austria Consort
Eela Craig
Julius Farmer
Uriah Heep
Hans Hollestalle
Pepe Lienhard
Little River Band
Hazy Osterwald
Niels Henning Orsted Pederson
P.F.M.
Mud
Shakin' Street
10 CC
Dave Pegg/Jethro Tull
Hans & Jan Vermeulen

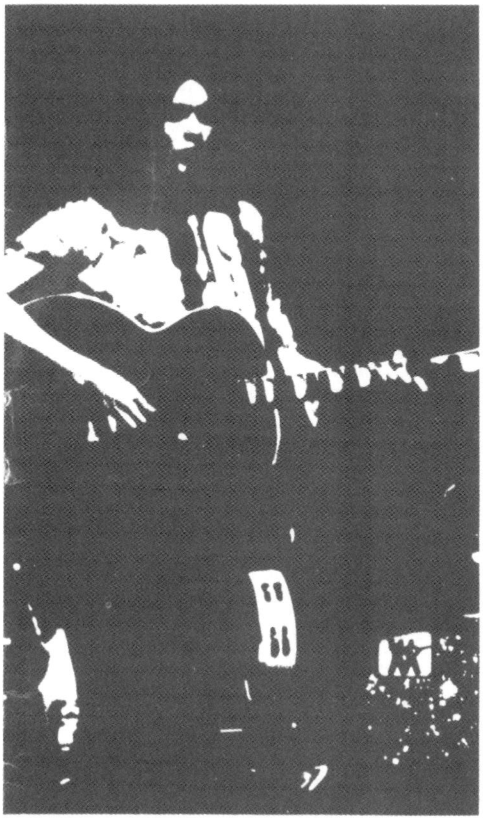

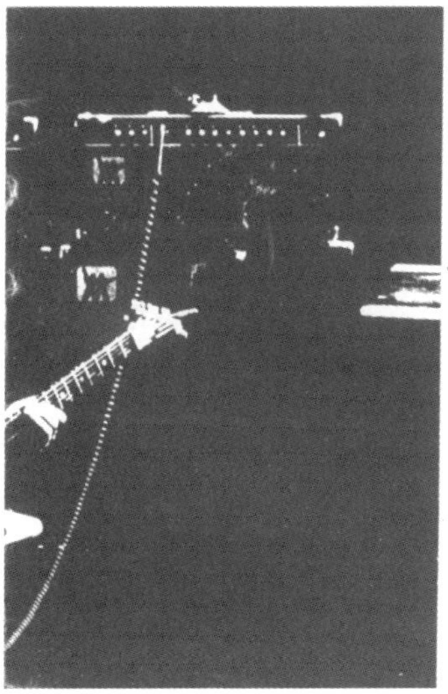

GUITAR

COWBOY GUITARS

by Steve Evans and Ron Middlebrook
foreword by Roy Rogers, Jr.

Back in the good old days, all of America was infatuated with the singing cowboys of movies and radio. This huge interest led to the production of "cowboy guitars." This fun, fact-filled book is an outstanding roundup of these wonderful instruments.

00000281 Softcover (232 pages) $35.00
00000303 Hardcover (234 pages) $55.00

ELECTRIC GUITAR CONSTRUCTION
A Guide for the First-Time Builder

by Tom Hirst

With this definitive book on building an electric guitar, you can create your own axe masterpiece, with the precise finish, the exact pickups, and the custom hardware you've always wanted. Organized logically from start to finish, this helpful guide will assist you every step of the way; from the design and planning stage to the final setup. Also includes a glossary of terms, an index of materials suppliers, and much more!

00000311 168 pages $39.95

New

THE GIBSON 'BURST
1958-1960

by Jay Scott and Vic DaPra
forewords by Jimmy Page and Robby Krieger

A musical instrument or a cultural icon? Certainly, the Gibson Les Paul "Sunburst" Standard has become the single most desirable and collectable electric guitar ever made. The late '50s middle-of-the-road guitar emerges as the turn-of-the-century Holy Grail. With over 300 'Bursts shown and 16 pages of full color photos, this is the book for all collectors. Also includes a 1958, '59, and '60 Sunburst Les Paul serial number list.

"Since the first publication of this book 'til today, the Sunburst has continued to inspire me and new generations of musicians. Thank you, Les." – Jimmy Page

00000423 Softcover $35.00
00000477 Hardcover $50.00

Centerstream@aol.com

New

THE GIBSON 335
Its History and Its Players

by Adrian Ingram

Gibson's first "semi-acoustic" the ES-335, which was neither totally solid nor fully acoustic, is the guitar of choice used by many famous guitarists such as Andy Summers, Elvin Bishop, Lee Ritenour, Jay Graydon, Robben Ford, Freddie King, John McLaughin, Jimmy Page, Chuck Berry, Tony Mottola, Johnny Rivers, Jack Wilkins, Bono, Grant Green, Eric Clapton, Stevie Ray Vaughan, Alvin Lee, B.B. King, Emily Remler, Otis Rush, Pete Townshend, John Lee Hooker, and Larry Carlton. This book includes the complete history of the 335, the players, a beautiful color section, chronology, shipping totals and more. A must-have for every 335 player and guitar enthusiast or collector!

00000353 120 pages $29.95

THE GIBSON L5

by Adrian Ingram

Introduced in 1922, the Gibson L5 is the precursor of the modern archtop guitar. This book takes a look at its history and most famous players, from its creation, through the Norlin years, to its standing today as the world's most popular jazz guitar. Includes a 16-page full-color photo section.

00000216 112 pages....................$29.95

GRETSCH – THE GUITARS OF THE FRED GRETSCH COMPANY

by Jay Scott

This comprehensive manual uncovers the history of Gretsch guitars through 32 pages of color photos, hundreds of black & white photos, and forewords by Fred Gretsch, George Harrison, Randy Bachman, Brian Setzer, and Duane Eddy. It covers each model in depth, including patent numbers and drawings for collectors.

00000142 286 pages $35.00

THE HAWAIIAN STEEL GUITAR AND ITS GREAT HAWAIIAN MUSICIANS

compiled & edited by Lorene Ruymar

This fascinating book takes a look at Hawaiian music; the origin of the steel guitar and how it spread throughout the world; Hawaiian playing styles, techniques and tunings; and more.

00000192 208 pages $34.95

THE HISTORY & ARTISTRY OF NATIONAL RESONATOR INSTRUMENTS

by Bob Brozman

This book is a history book, source book and owner's manual for players and fans that covers the facts and figures necessary for serious collectors. In addition to many black and white historical photos, there is a 32-page color section, and appendixes with serial numbers for all instruments, a company chronology, and a Hawaiian Artist Discography.

00000154 296 pages $35.00

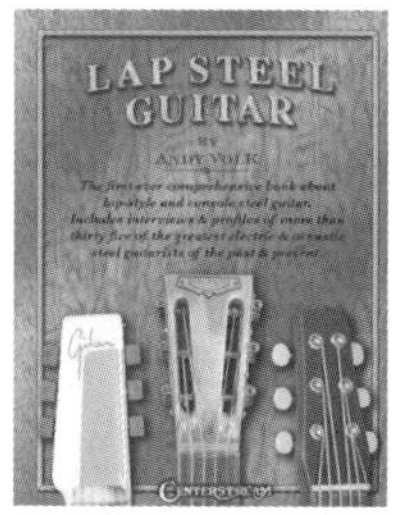

LAP STEEL GUITAR

by Andy Volk

This first-ever comprehensive book about lap-steel and console steel guitars includes: interviews and profiles of more than 35 of the greatest electric and acoustic steel guitarists of the past and present, representing most forms of music played in the world today. Also includes resources for guitars, amplifiers, accessories, instructional materials, steel guitar tunings; and much more.

00000320 336 pages $35.00

MAKING AN ARCHTOP GUITAR

by Robert Benedetto

The definitive work on the design and construction of an acoustic archtop guitar by one of the most talented luthiers of the twentieth century. Benedetto shows all aspects of construction, even through marketing your finished work. Includes a list of suppliers; a list of serial numbers for Benedetto guitars; full-color plates; photos from the author's personal scrapbook; and fold-out templates.

00000174 260 pages $39.95

RICKENBACKER

by Richard Smith

A complete and illustrated history of the development of Rickenbacker instruments from 1931 to the present, complete with information and full-color photos of the many Rickenbacker artists.

00000098 256 pages $35.00